The C and
UNIX Dictionary

The C and UNIX† Dictionary

From *Absolute Pathname* to *Zombie*

KAARE CHRISTIAN

The Rockefeller University
New York, New York

†UNIX is a trademark of AT&T Bell Laboratories.

QA 76.73
C15
C49
1988

WILEY

JOHN WILEY & SONS
New York • **Chichester** • **Brisbane** • **Toronto** • **Singapore**

Trademarks

UNIX, UNIX System III, and UNIX System V are trademarks of AT&T Bell Laboratories.
AT&T is a registered trademark of American Telephone and Telegraph.
CP/M is a trademark of Digital Research.
DEC, PDP, VAX, VMS, and VT are trademarks of Digital Equipment Corporation.
Ethernet is a trademark of Xerox Corporation.
IBM is a trademark of International Business Machines Corporation.
Intel is a trademark of Intel Corporation.
MS-DOS and Microsoft are registered trademarks of Microsoft Corporation.
PostScript is a trademark of Adobe Systems Incorporated.
Scribe and Unilogic are registered trademarks of Unilogic.
TEX is a trademark of the American Mathematical Society.
Xenix is a trademark of Microsoft Corporation.

Copyright © 1988 by John Wiley & Sons, Inc.

Library of Congress Cataloging in Publication Data:
Christian, Kaare, 1954-
    The C and UNIX dictionary / Kaare Christian.
       p.   cm.
    On t.p. the dagger symbol for trademark is superscript following
"UNIX" in the title.
    "From Absolute Pathname to Zombie."
    "A Wiley-Interscience publication."
    Bibliography: p.
    Includes index.
    ISBN 0-471-60929-3.
    ISBN 0-471-60931-5 (pbk.)
    1. C (Computer program language) 2. UNIX (Computer operating
system) I. Title.
QA76.73.C15C49 1988
005.26 — dc19
                                           88-14208
                                             CIP

Printed in the United States of America

10 9 8 7 6 5 4 3 2 1

For three kids
who have a lot of words to learn,
Kari, Arli, and Reed

CONTENTS

PREFACE

The importance of the UNIX system and the C programming language—their words, ideas, flavor, and style—is difficult to overstate. During my college career I was forced to punch (card decks), submit (jobs), and wait (for listings). It was not much fun. The generation after mine has had it much easier, thanks to Ken Thompson, Dennis Ritchie, William Joy, and others. Because of the UNIX system, it is much easier to get on with the job of using computers productively, for everyone's benefit.

Although the C language and the UNIX system have been evolving for over a decade, one of their most impressive characteristics is their stability. Over 90 percent of the definitions in this book could have been written in the mid to late 1970s. Of the remaining 10 percent, most relate either to ANSI C, to networking, or to workstations—the latest UNIX and C developments.

The approach that I have taken in most definitions is to move from the general to the more specific. When terms have a general usage plus a UNIX-specific usage, the first sentence of the definition usually tackles the general meaning, then the second places the term in a UNIX or C framework. When terms are only (or mostly) used in UNIX or C arenas, the definition tries to make that fact clear.

Another goal of mine is to show all definitions for each word, and to indicate which words are used as several parts of speech. Most definitions of verbs start with the word *to*; most of nouns start with *a* or *the*; and most of adjectives start with *pertaining* or *relating*. If a word has a similar sense when used as a noun and as a verb, only one of the definitions is likely to have much flesh.

Wherever it seemed appropriate, I have included additional information about words.

In many places I have supplied hints to help you pronounce abbreviations and other difficult terms.

I have often supplied brief histories for words with interesting or useful etymologies.

For many terms I have mentioned the names of relevant UNIX commands; more information can often be found in the reference manual citations for these commands.

Some definitions include an example dialogue or code fragment. In dialogues the part typed by the user is in a heavy typewriter typeface, while system response is in a lighter typeface. Thus in the following dialogue only the word pwd is typed by the user. (The $ is the system prompt, and the final underscore symbolizes the cursor on a video terminal.)

```
$ pwd
/usr1/kc
$ _
```

Although I can make no claims as a lexicographer, I have tried to be careful with the usage detailed here. In most cases I have tried to follow generally accepted usage in the UNIX and C worlds. To my eye, *filename*, *filesystem*, *pathname*, and *database* look best written as one word, although they are sometimes written as two words. *I-node* appears also in the literature as *inode* and *i node*, but I think the hyphen best implies its pronunciation. Of course, for each i-node there is an *i-node number*, which is another term that has been written in several styles. *Time-sharing* and *multi-user* also need a hyphen, while the other *multis* (processing, programming, tasking) are best written as a single word without a hyphen. The only case in which I consciously avoided the prevailing style is the word *superuser*. It is hyphenated in much of the UNIX literature, but if you look up other *superwords* in the dictionary you'll find few hyphens.

The cardinal rule for UNIX writers is that the word *UNIX* is never used as a noun (and obviously it's not much of a verb). Ask the lawyers about that one, but when writing about the UNIX system, always place a noun or noun phrase immediately after the word *UNIX*. This important dictum is ignored in most of the early UNIX literature, even that from Bell Laboratories, but it is followed in most recent writing. Of course in all writing about the UNIX system, mention should be made that UNIX is a trademark of AT&T Bell Laboratories.

Besides the mild prescriptions just listed, there are a few other suggestions scattered throughout the book. Most are tame. For example, *daemon* is preferred over *demon* for the computer set. Please don't ask why. Occasionally I've labeled a term as slang or informal; this often reflects my feeling that, like most slang terms, the usage varies, and each word means exactly what the speaker (or writer) wishes, no more and no less. If your favorite term is deprecated as slang but has a strict usage, please let me know.

Several reviewers have noticed a slight difference in complexity between the C definitions and the UNIX definitions. This reflects my perception of the needs of the readers. Most people searching for a definition of *current directory* have direct, pragmatic needs. Programmers, when reaching for a dictionary, often have more esoteric needs.

Deciding which *terms* to include was easy. Terms that relate to the UNIX system, to the C programming language, or that are commonly used in UNIX or C circles, are included. Deciding which *people* to include was much harder. Thousands have contributed to the UNIX system, and several dozen individuals have made very significant contributions. My approach has been to cite only those whose direct contribution to the development of the UNIX system are of the greatest importance, or those whose work in related fields has had a major impact. The obvious disadvantage of this approach is that most people already know of these individuals. It would be much more useful, in a reference work, to bring attention to many other individuals—people whose contributions are less well known but still of major importance.

I was astounded to discover that there are over a thousand terms in the UNIX and C lexicon. My initial letter to my editor suggested that there were approximately 400 UNIX and C terms, and I optimistically prophesied that there might be another hundred lurking in the shadows. It seems there were more shadows than I realized!

The first version of this book appeared as an appendix in the first edition of my book *The UNIX Operating System* (John Wiley & Sons, 1983). At that point the list was 12 pages long and contained 166 definitions. Some of the work on that list was done by my wife, Robin Raskin. While I was preparing the second edition of *The UNIX Operating System*, Cindy Jones expanded the original set of definitions considerably, to over 300 terms in about 40 pages. Cindy's work was thorough and precise and I appreciate her diligence. I then expanded everything about fourfold from there, completing the transition from an appendix to a book.

Please write if you have comments on this book. I am certain that there are additional words that should be included, and that there are terms whose definition could be improved. I can be reached at my permanent address, The Rockefeller University, Neurobiology

Laboratory, RU Box 138, 1230 York Avenue, New York, NY 10021, or cmcl2!rna!kc on the UUCP network. I look forward to your suggestions.

This book was written in Tübingen, West Germany, while I was on a leave of absence from The Rockefeller University. As I was not fluent in German, I was forced, almost hourly, to my Langenscheidts dictionary (Wörterbuch) to learn (or more often to relearn) a new word. It is ironic that during this period of intense reliance on one dictionary I was writing another. It remains to be seen if immersing yourself in one Gestalt while categorizing another is a good idea.

KAARE CHRISTIAN

Tübingen, West Germany
March 1988

The C and
UNIX Dictionary

absolute pathname A pathname that starts in the root directory. Absolute pathnames can always be distinguished from relative pathnames because absolute pathnames always start with the / character. An absolute pathname always refers to the same file, no matter where you are in the filesystem. For example, the absolute pathname '/usr1/kc/letters/janice.e' leads from the root directory, through the 'usr1', 'kc', and 'letters' directories, to the file 'janice.e'. *See also* pathname.

accent mark A mark that is placed near a letter, usually to indicate an altered pronunciation. For example, an umlaut, as in Tübingen. The standard `nroff/troff` macro packages contain character strings to produce accent marks, but the ability to actually print the accent mark depends on the capabilities of the printer.

access

To use the contents of a file, or the services of a computer or computer network. "I usually access the departmental UNIX system from my home."

The ability or right to use the contents of a file, or the services of a computer or computer network. Computer systems often have elaborate hardware and software safeguards to control access to resources. The UNIX system uses the login procedure to control access to user accounts, and it has a three-tiered file access system to control access to files and input/output I/O devices.

Pertaining to one's ability to use the contents of a file, and so on.

access mode   *See* file access mode; directory access mode.

access privilege   *See* file access mode.

access time   Time required to store or retrieve information from memory or mass storage. The average access time is one of the most important considerations when you are evaluating disk and memory peripherals.

account   An individual's resources on a machine. On UNIX systems, an individual is given an account by the system manager. This entails creating an entry in the '/etc/passwd' file, creating a home directory, and performing any other necessary chores.

acoustic coupler   An obsolete device that converts a serial data stream into audible telephone tones and vice versa so that they can be transmitted over the telephone system. The telephone handset must be manually fitted to the coupler each time a connection is made, thus acoustic couplers are not suitable for use by software such as uucp (a UNIX program that is the user interface to UUCP protocol). Also, acoustic couplers are limited to relatively low data rates, typically 300 baud. For these reasons direct connect modems have replaced most acoustic couplers. *See also* modem; direct-connect modem; serial communication.

actual arguments   The values that are supplied when a procedure is invoked. One procedure can be invoked with many different actual arguments. *See also* formal parameters.

actual group id   The group id of a user, as catalogued in the '/etc/passsswd' file. *See also* group id; effective group id.

actual user id   The user id of a user, as catalogued in the '/etc/passsswd' file. *See also* user id; effective user id.

adb   The universal UNIX debugger. adb helps a programmer to examine and patch binary files, set breakpoints, trace and single step a program, and examine core dumps.

address

A storage location in memory, on a disk, or on a computer network.

To access memory. For example, one might say "the operating system failed when it tried to address the third bank of memory." Also commonly used when people are talking about the amount of memory that a system can contain. "Running under DOS, a 286-based PC can address 1 megabyte of memory, but while running under Xenix, that same machine can address 16 megabytes of memory."

addressable cursor   A feature on most modern terminals that enables an application program to control the position of the cursor by sending control codes to the terminal. This feature is essential for screen-oriented applications software such as vi and emacs.

address of operator   A unary C language operator, symbolized by &, that returns the address of its operand. The operand must be an lvalue. You cannot use the address of operator to determine the address of a bit in a bitfield, a register variable, a constant, a function, or a label.

aggregate data type   An aggregate data type is one that has components. In C, the aggregate data types are arrays, structures, and unions. Aggregates are important because they make it possible for related information to be organized logically and accessed efficiently. Members of an aggregate data type are accessed by name for structures and unions and by an index expressions for arrays. There are some restrictions on aggregate data types—for example, in C there are no arithmetic or logical operations for aggregate data types, no assignment operation for the array type, and no initialization for auto (local to a function, and created when the function is invoked) aggregates.

AI (artificial intelligence)   A field of research that studies the construction of computer systems to perform activities that people would normally associate with human intelligence. For example, creating systems to aid in medical diagnosis, translate languages, understand languages, or provide expert advice within a given field of knowledge.

alarm   A settable software timer that, when it expires, sends a signal to a process. Alarms are used, for example, to timeout processes that otherwise might wait forever. The UNIX login process sets an alarm, so that it can abort the login if the user fails to complete the procedure.

algorithm   Step-by-step procedure for accomplishing a task.

alias

An alternate name for a command. *See also* argument list generation.

A built-in command of the C shell and Korn shell that is used to create and display aliases.

To create or use an alternate name. "I aliased *lwc* to *wc -l* because I often only want to count lines in a file."

alignment   The mapping of data types to specific address boundaries in a machine. Many machines have alignment requirements. Some others allow any alignment but operate more efficiently with optimal alignment. For example, characters are usually processed efficiently at any memory address, but two-byte integers often must be aligned on even addresses. Larger quantities, such as four-byte floating-point values, often must be aligned on four-byte boundaries. Because of alignment requirements, C language structures often contain holes. C language arrays are guaranteed not to contain holes, although the array elements may contain such holes. Some versions of C have compiler options that let the programmer control structure alignment.

ambiguous   Something that has more than one meaning. Ambiguous situations and systems are usually shunned in computer applications.

angle brackets   Either of the characters < or >. *See also* brackets.

ANSI C   A term used to describe any version of C that conforms to the specification written by the ANSI (American National Standards

Institute) X3J11 committee. Most of the revisions are extensions to Kernighan and Ritchie C that make it a more modern language, with more usage checking, more features to ensure portability, and a few additions that make C a more powerful language.

Additional keywords

const to declare items whose value does not change.

enum to declare enumerations; enumerations are not present in the original Kernighan and Ritchie definition, but have been present in most C compilers since before the ANSI standardization.

signed to explicitly declare data, especially characters, as signed.

void several uses; For instance, declaring generic pointers and functions with no return value.

volatile to specify that the compiler should not optimize code involving a given variable because it may be changed by outside events.

New operator and operations

unary plus to control expression evaluation

structure assignment to allow structures to be assigned, passed to functions and returned from functions. (This feature predates ANSI, but is not present in Kernighan and Ritchie C.)

Additional usage checking

function prototypes, which can specify function return values and argument types.

New preprocessor features

defined to detect previously defined identifiers in #if statements. (*defined* was not present in the Kernighan and Ritchie definition, although it was widely used before ANSI C.)

\# to stringize (covert an argument to a string) a macro argument.

\#\# to paste two macro arguments together.

\#error to produce error messages during compilation.

\#pragma to specify compiler options.

In addition, a minimal runtime library is specified.

Pronounced an-see. *See also* X3J11.

a.out   The default executable output file of the C compiler.

append   To place one one thing immediately after another. This term is often used in the UNIX text editors to signify placing one block of text after an existing block of text. In the C or Bourne shell, a command's standard output can be appended to an existing file using the >> I/O redirection symbol.

application program   Computer program for a specialized purpose, such as accounting, mailing, or data analysis.

archive

To make a copy of computer files for long-term storage.

A copy of computer files, usually stored on magnetic tape, intended for long-term storage.

A library. *See* library.

argc   The traditional name for the first parameter in the main procedure of a C language program. The first parameter always indicates the command line argument count; hence the name.

argument   Information that is passed to a command or subroutine to further direct its operation. *See also* argument, command line; argument, procedure.

argument, command line   UNIX command-line arguments are entered on the command line following the command name. Most UNIX command line arguments are option flags, which invoke alternate behavior of the command, or filenames. On a UNIX command line the command name and its arguments are separated from one another by spaces and/or tabs, and the command name always comes first. Because the command name always appears in position zero of the argument list, it is sometimes called the *zeroeth argument*. Because of the shell's argument list generation efforts, the arguments that you type on the command line are often transformed to something different by the time they are received by the program. *See also* option.

argument count   The number of arguments passed to a procedure or program. In a C program, the argument count is passed as the first parameter of the `main` routine, which is often named `argc`. In a Bourne shell program, the argument count is available in the `$#` shell variable. In a C shell program, the argument count is available in the `$argv` variable.

argument list generation   Transformation by the UNIX shell of command line information into final arguments. This procedure generally consists of command and parameter substitution, blank interpretation, and filename generation. The Berkeley and Korn shells contain additional argument list generation features, such as history substitution, tilde substitution, and aliases. For example, the following UNIX command invokes several argument list generation features:

```
$ echo $TERM `expr 2 + 2` j*.c
vt100 4 junk.c jiles.c john.c
$ _
```

The shell transforms the variable reference *$TERM* into its value, *vt100* (variable substitution); it executes the command *expr 2 + 2* and replaces it with its result, *4* (command substitution); and it produces an alphabetized list of files that start with the letter *j* and end with the pair of letters *.c* (filename generation). The resulting five words are then passed as arguments to the `echo` program, which writes them to the standard output. *See also* alias; blank interpretation; command substitution; filename generation; history, tilde substitution.

7

argument, procedure   Information that is passed to a procedure to enable it to perform its task. For example, the sin procedure computes the trigonometric sine of its argument. In the C language, arguments are in a comma-separated list, enclosed in parentheses, following the procedure name.

arguments, null   An argument to a program that is an empty string. The standard way of generating such an argument is to use a pair of double quotes, such as "", in a shell command line.

argument vector   The list of arguments for a program, as seen from within the program. The main procedure in a C language program can access the program's argument list using the procedure's second argument, which is often named argv. argv is a pointer to an array of pointers; each pointer in the array accesses one of the text strings in the argument vector.

argv   The traditional name for the second parameter in the main procedure of a C language program. The second parameter always is a pointer to an array (vector) of pointers to the command line arguments.

ARPANET   (Advanced Research Projects Agency Network) A wide area network developed to support defense industry projects. Various UNIX-based gateways exist so that authorized UNIX users access the ARPA network. *Pronounced* are-puh-net.

array   A data structure that provides an indexed set of contiguous data. The C language contains full features for arrays, as does the C shell. The Bourne shell does not contain array variables, although you can implement primitive array operations by using a separator character in an ordinary shell variable, as is done in the $PATH variable. The following is a C language declaration that creates an array called score that can store 100 characters.

```
char score[100];
```

See also record; data structure.

array bounds   The largest and smallest acceptable index for an array. In C, the lowest index of an array is always zero, and the highest is one less than the number of elements in the array. One of C's most dangerous features, albeit an occasionally useful feature, is its lack of checking of array indexes. For example, if X is an array of ten elements, X[-5] and X[100] are both valid expressions, although both are likely to cause problems during program execution. In a C shell script, referencing an out of bounds array element produces an error message such as *subscript out of bounds*.

array, multidimensional   An array whose elements are themselves arrays; an array of arrays. One subscript expression is needed for each dimension of the array. A one-dimensional array is sometimes called a *vector*; a two-dimensional array is sometimes called a *matrix*.

ASCII   American Standard Code for Information Interchange. A standard character code used with many computers and data terminals for data transfer and storage. ASCII defines an internal binary representation of characters. The UNIX system was developed and first used on computers that supported ASCII, and many remnants of ASCII usage persist in the UNIX system, although efforts are under way to support European and Asian character sets. *Pronounced* asc-key. *See also* EBCDIC.

ASCII chauvinism   The unthinking assumption that all systems use the ASCII character code. The UNIX system has many examples of ASCII chauvinism.

assembler   A program that converts assembly language programs into machine code. UNIX systems traditionally contain a very simple assembler because most assembly code on UNIX systems comes from the C compiler, not from assembly language programmers. *See also* macro; macro assembler.

assembly language   A programming language that relates directly to the native instruction set of a particular computer. In UNIX systems, assembly language programs are occasionally used in situations requiring efficiency. The disadvantages of assembly language programming are that such programs are difficult to write and maintain and are not transportable from one type of computer to another. Most compilers on UNIX systems emit assembly language near the end of the compilation process.

assignment   In a programming language, an operation that stores a value in a variable. In the Bourne shell and the C language, assignment is specified by the = symbol. The value to the right of the = is stored in the variable (C lvalue) to the left of the = operator. In the C shell, assignment is performed by the set command. *See also* operator, assignment.

associative array   An array whose indices are strings of text, rather than numbers. Unlike ordinary arrays, associative arrays do not have an implied ordering, but they are much more flexible than ordinary arrays. The awk program has associative arrays.

automatic variables   Variables that are automatically created when the function where they exist is called and that are automatically destroyed when that function exits. In C this is called the auto storage class. Also called *dynamic variables*. *See* storage class, auto.

auto storage class   *See* storage class, auto.

awk   A programming language developed to manipulate text files. awk programs consist of (enhanced) ed style regular expressions, each coupled to a code fragment. Each time a line of the input matches a regular expression, the code fragment is executed. The language was developed by (and its name taken from the initials of) A. Aho, P. J. Weinberger, and B. W. Kernighan.

B

B   A systems programming language, designed by Ken Thompson, that was the model for Dennis Ritchie's C language. B featured just two data types, words, and pointers to words. B was heavily influenced by Martin Richards's BCPL.

backend   The part of a computer application that deals mostly with data manipulation, unlike the frontend, which manages user dialogues and acquires data. The backend of a compiler is the code generator. The backend of a database management system is the part that manages data storage and retrieval. *See also* frontend.

background

. A metaphorical place in the UNIX system where processes live when they are not interacting with a terminal. You can run a process in the background by placing an ampersand at the end of the command line. In traditional UNIX systems, processes are either in the background or the foreground for their lifetime. In newer systems, that feature job control, it is possible to move a process from foreground to background. Berkeley UNIX has the bg and fg commands to make a stopped processes start executing in either the background or the foreground. *See also* foreground; job control.

To place a process in the background, as in "When I saw the message on my screen that I had received new mail, I backgrounded the editor and then read my mail."

Pertaining to something in the background.

background process   A process that runs unattended (not interacting with a terminal) in a manner such that other programs may be initiated and interacted with while the background process is running. Some background processes are started during the UNIX system bootstrap to perform system management functions; other background processes are started interactively by placing an ampersand at the end of the command line.

backquote   The character `` ` ``. When you surround a portion of a shell command line in backquotes, that portion is executed as a command, and the output of the command is inserted in the command line. This process is called *command substitution. See also* command substitution.

backslash   The character \. On a shell command line, when you precede a character with a backslash it loses its special meaning. For example, the command ls *.c lists all files whose extension is *.c*, but the command ls *.c lists the file named *.c*. The backslash has the meaning *quote next character* in several UNIX contexts, including the shell and the standard editors. It is the line continuation character in the C programming language, and it introduces C escape sequences.

backup

To copy files to secondary storage for use in case the originals are damaged or lost. Backups are performed periodically by the management of most large systems; they must be performed by individual users on small systems. "Please backup the system tomorrow tonight at ten."

A disk or tape containing files for archival purposes. "The most recent backup was accidentally erased by our new operator."

The act of making a backup. "Tomorrow the operator will perform the monthly backup."

basename

The name of a file, when stripped of its extension (the period, if any, and all that follows). For example, the basename of 'histochem.c' is 'histochem'. *See also* extension.

A UNIX command that extracts the basename from a filename.

batch processing   Noninteractive data processing. In a batch system, programs are submitted by users to the computer for subsequent execution, pending scheduling by human operators or the operating system. The scheduling may introduce a considerable delay (often hours) between the time a program is introduced to the system and the time that program actually starts to execute, as a consequence of operating system rules for optimizing machine utilization. The UNIX system is not a batch system, although subsystems have been built to create batch facilities within the UNIX realms. *See also* interactive computer system.

baud rate   Transmission speed between computers and/or electronic communication equipment or devices, measured in bits per second. The baud rate divided by 10 is a rough measure of the characters transmitted per second. Modems that operate over voice-grade telephone lines usually operate at 1200 or 2400 baud. Hardwired terminals often operate at 4800, 9600, or 19,200 baud. Local area networks typically operate at over a million baud.

BCPL   A systems programming language, designed by Martin Richards, that was the model for Ken Thompson's B language.

bdevsw   A data structure in the UNIX kernel. bdevsw is a table of addresses of device driver routines to manage block devices. The major device number of a block special file is actually an index into this table. When you create new block special files, using the mknod program, you must determine the device's major device number, often by looking at the source code for the bdevsw table. *See also* cdevsw; data structure.

Belle   A computer system for playing chess, developed by Ken Thompson and Joe Condon. Belle at one time was the world champion chess system.

Bell Laboratories   The research organization for AT&T (American Telephone & Telegraph) and the birthplace of UNIX.

benchmark

A process that can be followed to evaluate a system. For example, the *Whetstone* benchmark evaluates the floating-point performance of a system.

To evaluate a system. "We benchmarked the new system at twice the performance of a VAX 11/780."

Berkeley 2.x   The 16-bit, PDP-11 version of Berkeley UNIX. The *x* is the release number. For example, Berkeley 2.9 was one of the last versions of Berkeley UNIX to support 16-bit computers. Also 2BSD; 2.*x*BSD.

Berkeley 4.x   The version of UNIX supported by the University of California at Berkeley. The 4 signifies the 32-bit, virtual memory version of the system, while the digit following the decimal point is the release number. Berkeley 4.1 and 4.2 were originally designed to work on Digital Equipment Corporation VAX computers, although these systems were widely ported to other computer architectures, such as the Motorola MC68000. Also 4BSD; 4.*x*BSD.

Berkeley UNIX   A generic term used to refer to the version of UNIX created at the University of California at Berkeley. *See also* BSD; Berkeley 2.9; Berkeley 4.x.

bin   A directory that contains executable software. Traditionally, there have been two bins on UNIX systems, '/bin' and '/usr/bin', although many systems have additional bins to meet specific requirements. Many individuals create their own bins, such as '/usr/kc/bin' for kc's private collection of executable software. The name is derived from the word binary because most of the files in a bin directory are binaries. However, the customary meaning of bin, which is a place where things are stored, is also appropriate.

binary

An executable file containing a machine language program. (Not an executable file containing a shell script.) The names of the standard directories for UNIX executable files, '/bin' and '/usr/bin', are taken from this term. Note that many of the programs in '/bin' and '/usr/bin' are not binaries; rather, they are command scripts (text files). Usage note. The term *binary*, in reference to files, is usually reserved for *executable* files. For example, "the binary for the date command was corrupted in yesterday's power surge." The term *binary file* is often used to refer to *data* files, although it can be used to refer to an executable file. For example, "the comets database is stored in a massive binary file."

Pertaining to the base two number system. In a binary number system the sole digits are zero and one (rather than zero through nine, as in the decimal system). Binary is important for computers because computers are constructed from logic elements that take on one of two states, corresponding to the binary digits zero and one.

Data that is not text and that contains codes that are not printable.

binary file   A file, usually containing data, that contains codes that are not part of the ASCII character set; an ordinary file that is not a text file. Binary files can utilize all 256 possible values for each byte in the file. Unfortunately, they cannot be typed on a terminal because most of the 256 values are not printable ASCII characters. Binary files can be examined using the od (octal dump) program, which converts binary codes into printable ASCII equivalents.

binary license   A license that a software user acquires from a software vendor that entitles the user to run a particular software package, using executable files provided by the vendor. It does not entitle the user to a copy of the source code for that package. Limited source code is sometimes supplied with binary licensed software, so that the software can be configured to meet the customer's needs. *See also* source license.

binary operator   An arithmetic, logical, or other operator that requires two operands (two values on which to operate). For example, the addition operator, which is usually written as +, requires two operands, as in x + y. In C most operators are either binary, or unary. C has only one higher-order (tertiary) operator, the conditional operator. *See also* unary operator.

bit   Binary digit (zero or one), the smallest unit of data.

bit block   A group of bits. The term usually refers to a group of bits in a graphic display buffer that correspond to some region on the display screen.

BITBLT   A hardware device (or a software routine) that can rapidly move information from one place in a raster display to another location. The term is derived from the phrase *bit block transfer* (a bit block is a region of a raster display). *Pronounced* bit blit. *See also* raster graphics.

bit bucket   A place where output can be sent to be discarded. The UNIX system bit bucket is a character special file named '/dev/null'. The UNIX bit bucket can also be read, which immediately produces an end-of-file condition. *See also* null device.

bit field   A bit field is a C language feature that allows you to conveniently access individual bit positions in a word. Bit fields are declared as part of a structure; thus, syntactically they appear as structure members. Bit fields are often used to access predefined bits in hardware device registers.

bitmap   Most generally, an array of bits. Usually the bits are in a display memory of a raster display device. Modifying the data in the bitmap alters the picture on the display. The *map* in the word *bitmap* refers to the relationship between locations in the array of bits and locations on the screen. Most graphics workstations contain a bitmap, which is written by the software to produce output on the screen.

bitwise operator   An operator that performs Boolean operations simultaneously on all the bits in its operands, unlike a conventional Boolean (logical) operator, which interprets each operand as a logical true or false, and then produces a corresponding result. The C language has four bitwise operators: AND (&), OR (|), NOT (˜), and exclusive OR (ˆ). In C, the expression 1 & 2 is 0, and 1 | 2 is 3. The similar-looking logical expressions produce very different results: 1 && 2 is true (1) and 1 || 2 is also true (1).

blank interpretation   The phase of the shell's argument list generation process during which the (blank separated) words of a command line are separated into arguments. Quoting can be used to create arguments with internal spaces.

block

In a programming language, a region of a program. In C, the body of a function is a block, and any group of statements surrounded by braces is a block. C blocks can have local data declarations and definitions, and blocks within a function can be used wherever a single statement is appropriate. Also called a *compound statement.*

On a disk or tape, a group of data (usually a group of 512 or 1024 bytes) that is transferred as a unit.

To enter a waiting state. "When a process issues a read request, it blocks until that request is fulfilled."

block device   An I/O peripheral that is capable of storing a UNIX filesystem. Block devices are normally accessed via block special files, although most block devices are also capable of being accessed via a character special file, usually for system management purposes. Typical block devices are disks and tapes.

blocking factor   A software transfer size that is used to access a device, usually a tape. Blocking factors must usually be a multiple of the inherent block size of the device.

block special file   A UNIX special file that provides an interface to a device capable of supporting a filesystem. *See also* special file; device file; block device.

Boolean   A variable that has a true/false value. Named after George Boole, who was the first person to develop an algebra based on values of true and false. The Bourne shell does not have Boolean variables, although in the shell the value 0 customarily represents true and other values represent false. This custom stems from the fact that programs that exit without encountering problems return a zero exit status (true) and programs that encounter problems return a nonzero error code (false). The C programming language also does not have a Boolean data type. C has adopted the opposite convention: zero represents false and any other value represents true. The Pascal language has a true Boolean data type.

boot   To make the transition from a powered down, or nonoperational state, to a functional state.

bootblock   The first block of a filesystem. The name refers to the common UNIX usage of the bootblock, which is to store a short bootstrap program. *See also* superblock.

booting   Said of a system that is performing initialization and other tasks that must be completed before the system can perform ordinary tasks. In the UNIX system there is an early boot phase, which loads in the operating system kernel, initializes memory, and results in a single-user operation. This phase of booting typically takes less than a minute. The second phase is the transition from single-user operation to multi-user operation. The tasks performed during this phase are catalogued in the '/etc/rc' initialization shell script. They typically include filesystem consistency checks, execution of background daemons, and filesystem mounting. The time required for this second phase varies widely; on systems with multiple large disks that must be checked, this process can take many minutes. The first phase is often called *booting single-user*, and the second phase is sometimes called *booting multi-user*.

bootstrap program   A short program that can be easily loaded by hardware, usually just following power on or system reset. For example, the UNIX system commonly stores bootstrap programs on the first block of a disk. On UNIX systems the purpose of the bootstrap program is to load the kernel from a disk file, which is usually called '/unix', '/xenix', '/vmunix', or something similar. To perform this function, the bootstrap program must possess rudimentary knowledge of the disk-drive hardware, UNIX directory files, and UNIX i-nodes.

Bourne shell   Shell program used in Version 7, System V, and Berkeley UNIX Systems; named after its author, S. R. Bourne. The Bourne shell is the most widely available UNIX shell; thus, it is almost universally used to develop scripts that are widely distributed. However, the interactive features of the Bourne shell are not as advanced as those of the C shell or the (Bourne compatible) Korn shell. Thus many UNIX users learn two separate shells, one for writing portable scripts and one for interactive use. *See also* shell.

Bourne, Steven R.   Author of the Bourne shell.

brace   One of the characters { or }. Used in the C language to surround blocks. Used in the Bourne shell to surround groups of commands that should be executed as a group. Used in the C shell to surround variable names, and also to force expansion of the items in a comma separated list. Also called *curly brace*. Note, often confused with the term *bracket*.

bracket

Most generally, a square bracket, an angle bracket, a parenthesis, a curly brace, or another grouping character. *See also* parenthesis; angle bracket; brace.

More specifically, either of the characters [or]. Used in the C language and the C shell to enclose array indices. Used in Bourne shell, C shell, and editor regular expressions to enclose character sets. Also called a *square bracket*. *Note:* often confused with the term *brace*.

To place something within braces, parentheses, brackets, or other grouping symbols.

branch

In a program, to interrupt the normal sequential flow of instructions and instead execute a nonsequential instruction.

One of several possible instruction sequences in a program.

break key   Key on the terminal keyboard that sends an unmistakable code (recognizable at any baud rate) to the host computer. During the login process the break key may cause the UNIX system to change its communication speed in an attempt to synchronize speeds with the user's particular terminal.

breakpoint   A code in an executable program image that, when executed, returns control to a debugger. Debuggers such as adb, dbx, and sdb can insert and remove breakpoints from programs under test.

break statement   In the Bourne shell, a statement that terminates the innermost enclosing for, while, or until loop. Execution next occurs at the first statement following the end of the loop. In the C shell, a statement that terminates the innermost enclosing foreach or while statement. Execution resumes at the first statement following the end of the loop. In the C language, a break statement terminates the innermost enclosing do, for, while, or switch statement. Execution resumes at the statement following the end of the innermost loop. break (or continue) is required in switch statements if you want each case to be distinct; without breaks each case flows into the following.

breaksw   In the C shell, a statement that marks the end of a case statement within a switch. Without a breaksw, each case falls through to the next.

break, troff   An interruption in the text filling process that causes the currently collected text to be output. Subsequent text is formatted starting on a new line. Breaks are caused by numerous commands, including the .sp (extra vertical space) and .br (force a break) commands. Breaks are also caused by any lines in a troff document that start with white space.

BSD   Berkeley Software Distribution. *See* Berkeley UNIX.

BSS region   The section of a process image that contains uninitialized data. In the UNIX system, such data is guaranteed to be initialized to a pattern of all bits off. The size of a program's BSS region is printed by the size program. *See also* text region; data region.

buffer

A temporary data storage location. Buffers are used in many places in computer systems, in both hardware and software. The most important buffers in the UNIX system are the buffers maintained by the kernel to mediate between processes and I/O devices. The kernel's buffers for disks (block devices) are called *block buffers*, and those for terminals (character devices) are called *c-lists*. *See also* buffered I/O.

To temporarily store data as it is being sent or received. The purpose is usually to increase efficiency, or to meet specific I/O device requirements, such as the common disk requirement for transfers of blocks of data.

buffered I/O   Buffers are usually employed to make I/O more efficient. Instead of performing many small transfers, one larger transfer is performed each time the buffer is full. The UNIX kernel contains buffers to manage the data flow between it and I/O devices. However, the term *buffered I/O* usually refers to the buffers that are contained in a program to buffer the transactions between the program and the UNIX kernel. The C language contains a subroutine library called the *standard I/O library* to enable C programs to conveniently take advantage of buffered I/O. *See also* buffer; portable C I/O library.

bug   Error in a computer program or in the computer hardware. (Informal.)

built-in command   A command that is executed directly by the shell, rather than by having the shell exec a child process. For example, the cd command must be executed by the shell itself; it would do little good for a child process to change directory and then exit. One of the strengths of the UNIX system is the fact that the shell's built-in commands are executed using the same syntax as that for external commands.

bus error   A condition that arises when a program attempts to perform an operation that the computer hardware is unable to perform. The most common example comes from the PDP-11, where using a pointer with its low bit set to access a two-byte quantity generates a bus error. When a bus error occurs, the process receives the bus error signal. The usual result is that the program aborts with a core dump.

byte   Group of bits; typically a set of eight bits. Most of the mass storage devices and I/O devices available today are designed to transfer sequences of eight-bit bytes. On most systems a byte is large enough to hold a single ASCII character; thus, the size of an ASCII text file in bytes is usually the same as its length in characters.

C

C   *See* C language.

C++   A programming language developed by Bjarne Stroustrup of Bell Laboratories. C++ is an extension of C. Added features include the ability to create new data types and to assign different meanings to operators, which is called *operator overloading.* C++ also pioneered some of the features that have been added to ANSI C, such as function prototypes. *Pronounced* see-plus-plus.

call

To activate a procedure, function, or program. In most languages it is possible to pass information (arguments) to the callee and to receive values back (return values). When a call instruction or command is executed, execution at the current location is suspended; instead the called procedure (or function or program) is executed. When the called entity is finished, it returns, causing execution to resume at the location following the original call.

The process of activating a procedure, function, or program.

call by reference   A feature of many programming languages, such as Pascal, that allows you to pass a reference to a variable to a called procedure or function. Then during the execution of the called procedure or function, it can alter the value of the referenced variable. In Pascal it is not possible to pass constants or expressions by reference. Most languages that have call by reference also have another calling convention, such as call by value.

call by value   A feature of many programming languages, such as C and Pascal, that allows you to pass a value to a called procedure or function. Changes made to the value within the called procedure or function do not affect the original information. The C language is an interesting example because it is limited to a call by value procedure interface. However, in C it is possible to achieve the effect of call by reference by passing the address of an lvalue.

call graph   A text or graphic display showing the procedure call record of a program.

canonical   The standard method of doing something. In the UNIX system the term often refers to the standard processing of special characters by the tty handler.

carriage return   Keyboard character or character code that is often used as an end of line or end of command delimiter. The name is derived from typewriters, which contain an analogous key that returns the carriage to the initial position on a line. Labeled *Return* or *Enter* on most keyboards. Equivalent to Ctrl-M. On many micro-computer systems, lines of text in text files are delimited with carriage returns or carriage return, newline pairs. When such files are transferred to UNIX systems, the end-of-line markers must be translated to newlines, which are the standard line delimiters for UNIX text files.

case

The capitalization, either upper or lower, of a letter.

A conditional statement in the Bourne shell. *See also* case statement.

A keyword used to mark each label in a C shell `switch` statement.

case insensitive   Pertaining to a system or program that ignores the case of letters in certain situations. For example, the MS-DOS system ignores case in command names and filenames, and the Pascal programming language ignores case in identifiers.

case sensitive   Pertaining to a system or program where case matters. For example, the UNIX system is case sensitive in most matters, and the C language is always case sensitive.

case statement   A Bourne shell statement that executes one of a series of alternatives; a one-of-*n*-way branch. Each alternative in the case statement is identified by a case label. Alternatives are chosen on the basis of pattern matching, and the case labels may contain metacharacters. Analogous to the C language switch statement. Also, a C language statement that acts as a label for one of the alternatives in a C switch statement. Each case label contains a constant expression, and if the value of the expression in the enclosing switch statement matches the value in the case label, the statements following the case is executed. *See also* case.

case labels

In the Bourne shell, the patterns that label the alternatives in a case statement. Each pattern may contain metacharacters, and a case label can consist of several alternative patterns.

In the C shell, the strings that label each alternative.

In C, the labels for a switch statement.

cast

To convert a value of one type to a another type by explicitly indicating the type conversion using a cast operator.

A conversion of a value from one type to another.

cast operator   A C language unary operator that specifically indicates a type conversion of the operand to its right. A C cast is written by placing a parenthesized type name to the left of an operand. The operand is then converted to the given type, as if it had been assigned to a variable of the given type.

cathode ray tube (CRT)   *See* CRT.

cbreak mode   An operational mode of the Berkeley tty handler that enables a program to receive each character as it is typed, yet still enables the user to use the interrupt and quit characters for their customary purpose. A compromise between normal (cooked) mode and raw mode. *See also* cooked mode; raw mode.

cd

A built-in command on the Bourne, Korn, and C shells that allows the user to move from one directory to another. cd stands for *change directory*. Some shells interrogate the $CDPATH variable to make it easier to move to non-local directories. *Pronounced* see-dee. *See also* change directory; pwd.

To move to another directory.

cdevsw   A data structure in the UNIX kernel. cdevsw is a table of addresses of device driver routines that manage character I/O devices. The major device number of a character special file is actually an index into this table. When you create new character special files, using the mknod program, you must determine the device's major device number, often by looking at the source code for the cdevsw table. *See also* bdevsw; data structure.

$CDPATH   A variable in modern versions of the Bourne shell that allows you to specify a list of directories whose subdirectories you often visit. When you issue a cd command, each of the directories in the $CDPATH are searched until the desired directory is found. The $CDPATH is to the cd command, as the $PATH variable is to executing programs.

change directory   To move from one directory to another. *See also* cd.

character   Symbol generally corresponding to a key on a terminal keyboard. Characters can be alphanumerics, punctuation marks, or other special symbols. Characters are usually stored in a single byte. The most common character coding system on UNIX systems is ASCII, although the UNIX system also is available on computers using EBCDIC.

character device   An I/O peripheral that is used primarily for transferring groups of characters at a time. Typical character devices are terminals, communications links, and some specialized

25

devices, such as data collection peripherals and graphics peripherals. Such devices are accessed via a character special file.

character set

The binary coding system used for characters on a particular machine. The two common character sets are ASCII and EBCDIC. *See also* ASCII, EBCDIC.

An element of a regular expression. Character sets are available in the standard UNIX text editors and in the shell's filename generation process. By enclosing a group of characters in square brackets, you create a character set. In a matching situation, the match succeeds if the character in the corresponding position of the target string appears in the character set. For example, the regular expression *th[aei]n* matches any of the text strings *than*, *then*, or *thin*. The shell command 1s -1 *.[cfs] displays a long format listing of all files in the current directory whose names end in .c, .f, or .s. To negate a shell character set (i.e., to match any character not given in the set), place an exclamation point immediately following the opening square bracket. For example, the shell command 1s -1 *[!c] displays a long format listing of all files in the current directory whose names end in something other than the letter *c*. You can also mention a range of characters in a character set by placing a hyphen between the characters at the extreme of the range. For example, the shell command 1s [A-Z]* lists all files in the current directory that start with a capital letter. *See also* regular expression.

character-erase character   *See* erase character.

character special file   Special file that provides an interface to an I/O device. The character interface is used for devices that cannot support a filesystem and as an alternate interface to devices capable of supporting a filesystem. When a program sends data to (or receives data from) a special file, the kernel actually transfers the data to a hardware device. Data is not actually stored in character special files; rather, it exists so that programs can easily transfer data to/from hardware devices. Special files are a part of the filesystem; thus, they can be listed using the 1s program. If you make a long-form display (1s -1) of a character special file, the first letter in the type/mode field is *c*. Most special files are housed in the '/dev' directory. Some of the most important character special files are '/dev/console (the system console), '/dev/tty' (your terminal), '/dev/null' (the null device), '/dev/mem' (memory; also files for terminals). *See also* special file; device file.

char type   A C language data type that can store a single character. There are two types: signed and unsigned. In C, the char type is considered an integral type, and all operators that can be applied to integers can also be applied to chars.

chdir

An archaic name for the cd command. *See* cd.

To move to another directory.

child process   A UNIX process can split into two (replicate itself) using the fork system call. Following the fork, the invoking process is called the *parent process* and the offspring is called the *child*. Process lineage is important in UNIX for several reasons. One reason is that pipes can only be created between closely related processes. Another reason is that the UNIX software signals work within process groups, and processes in a process group are usually closely related. *See also* fork; parent process.

chip   Small electronic device, fabricated by means of semiconductor technology, and containing more than one element in a single package. Chips are miniature electrical circuits which are the building blocks of modern computers. (Sometimes called *bugs* because of their appearance, but this usage does not refer to errors.)

cipher text   The encoded form of a message. Also called *encrypted text*. *See also* clear text.

C language   A general-purpose programming language that is the primary language underlying the UNIX system. Also called C. It has been classified as a middle-level language. C has been praised for its economy of expression, absence of restrictions, and generality. C was developed by D. M. Ritchie in the early 1970s, and it was first described in the book *The C Programming Language*, which Ritchie coauthored with Brian Kernighan. In the late 1970s Ritchie authorized several small changes to the standard described in the book. In the mid 1980s the language was extended and standardized by the ANSI X3J11 committee. Although C and UNIX were once inseparable, C has now become a widely used language on virtually all computer systems, especially on microcomputer systems. The name *C* naturally follows *B*, which is an earlier language designed by Ken Thompson.

clear text   The unencoded version of a message. An encryption program, such as the UNIX system's crypt program, converts an unencoded file into cipher text. Given the proper password, it is possible to convert the cipher text back into clear text. *See also* cipher text.

clist   A data structure in the UNIX kernel that is used to store data coming from, or going to, terminals. Each individual clist can house a small number of characters, For example, 32, but multiple clists can be chained together to store hundreds of characters. The advantage of using clists instead of just setting aside a fixed amount of storage for each communication line is flexibility; with clists the storage can be dynamically assigned as needed. clists that are not currently in use are linked into a list of available clists.

code

An informal term for software. Usually refers to source code. *See also* source code.

To write software.

A particular bit pattern that represents a certain value or character. For example, the ASCII code defines a set of bit patterns for most common characters.

code fragment   An incomplete piece of software source code, usually used to illustrate an idea.

code generation   A phase of the compilation process during which a program is translated into a particular machine or assembly language. The preprocessing and syntactical analysis stages of a compiler can be programmed similarly on various machines, but the code generation phase must be individually crafted for each type of machine.

code generator   The part of a compiler that generates the machine-dependent code. Also called the *backend*.

coerce   To force a variable or expression to assume another type.

coercion, type   Forcing a variable declared as one type to be interpreted or used as another type. *See also* cast.

collide   For two or more messages to be placed simultaneously onto a communication path. *See also* collision.

collision   An interference of one message with another, on certain types of communication media. For example, it is possible for collisions to occur on the Ethernet because two senders might simultaneously sense that the network is free, and then simultaneously start a transmission. The Ethernet is designed so that all collisions are detected and then retransmitted. The Ethernet designers felt that detecting and repairing collisions was simpler and more effective than providing a means for avoiding collisions.

command

An order directing the system to perform some operation. Most UNIX commands are carried out by the UNIX shell, by either performing the command internally or executing a program.

Note: In nontechnical usage the word *command* can be used as a verb. This is not recommended in reference to entering computer commands; even gurus don't command the system to list their files.

command file   Ordinary text file containing commands, usually shell commands. Also called a *shell script* or *shell program*.

command interpreter   The component of an operating system that decodes and executes commands entered by the user. The UNIX system command interpreter is called the *shell*, and in UNIX jargon the two terms are almost synonymous. There are several widely used shells, including the universally available *Bourne* shell and the Berkeley *C Shell*. *See also* Bourne shell; C shell; Korn shell; shell.

command language   System of commands for use in controlling an interactive computer system. The UNIX command languages are heavily indebted to the Version 6 UNIX shell, which contained variables, a very simple flow of control statement, and a mechanism for expanding words such as **.c* into a list of files whose names end in *.c* (filename generation).

command line   A line of input containing one or more commands, such as a command to the UNIX shell. Multiple commands in the UNIX system may either be independent (separated by ; or &) or joined together in a pipeline (separated by |).

command mode   A mode of many interactive programs, during which commands may be entered. When these programs are not in command mode, it is typical for data entry to take place. The UNIX text editors ed, ex, and vi all have a command mode. *See also* modeless; text entry mode.

command name   When you type in a command, the first word on the line is usually the name of a command. Words following the command name are called arguments. Sometimes the command name is referred to as the zeroeth argument because it is the first word in the argument list, followed by the "true" arguments numbered consecutively beginning with the number one.

command substitution   Replacement of a command enclosed in backquotes by the text resulting from the execution of that command. For example, in the following dialogue the output of the ls ... wc pipeline becomes part of the text of the echo command.

```
$ ls *.c
calc.c      do_corr.c  do_hist.c
event.c     grhist.c   hist.c
junk.c      lem.c      ohelp.c
$ echo There are `ls *.c | wc -l` .c files here.
There are 9 .c files here.
$ _
```

When the shell acquires the command shown above, its first chore is to execute the `ls *.c | wc -l` command. Then the output from that command, 9, is conceptually placed in the echo command to create the following: echo There are 9 .c files here. Finally the echo command is executed with its six arguments, and the result is as shown above.

Another common use of command substitution is do arithmetic operations with shell variables.

```
$ i=15
$ i=`expr $i + 1`
$ echo $i
16
$ _
```

See also argument list generation; backquotes.

comma operator   *See* operator, comma.

comment   A region of a program or command script that is ignored by the language interpreter or compiler. They exist so that people can embed information, such as a description of an algorithm, that is useful to humans but not to the machine. In the shell programming language the # signifies the start of a comment, which extends to the end of a line. In the C language comments are enclosed in /* and */ brackets, and they can be more than one line long.

comment out   To make part of a program into a comment, usually for testing. Regions of a program are often commented out temporarily, and then restored. Commenting out is preferred to deleting the material, because it facilitates reentry of the commented-out material. "Comment out the file access test and see if the error message disappears."

compact   To reduce the size of a file without losing any of the information in the file. Archival text files are often compacted to save space. A complementary operation is used to restore the file to its original form.

compile   To translate a program written in a high level language into machine language form that can be directly executed on a computer.

compiler   A computer program that translates a text file containing a program written in a high-level programming language into machine language output. On UNIX systems the machine language output from a compiler is called an *object file*. Before an object file can be executed, it must be linked with other object files by ld, the UNIX linkage editor (linker). On UNIX systems the compiler often invokes ld directly.

compiler compiler   A program that translates a description of a grammar into a program that can recognize that grammar. The term comes from the fact that recognizing a grammar is one of the main elements of a traditional compiler; thus, a program that translates a description of a compiler into a compiler is called a *compiler compiler*. The UNIX system's compiler compiler is yacc, whose name stands for *yet another compiler compiler. See also* yacc.

compile time   A reference to things that happen during compilation, or things that can be accomplished during compilation. "We can't initialize that array at compile time, because it's contents are in a separate file."

compound statement   *See* block.

compress   *See* compact.

computer   A machine that can perform various arithmetic, logical, and flow-of-control instructions at a high rate of speed. The result is usually the transformation of information and/or the control of electromechanical systems and instruments. Modern computers are based on electronic technology. The UNIX system is an operating system that runs on many midsize computers.

computer-aided instruction   Using a computer for teaching purposes. The UNIX system has the learn program, which can teach you how to use some of the most important UNIX facilities.

concatenate   To combine one thing (often a file or a string) after another. The cat program was named for this operation; it can concatenate its input files. The C language contains the strcat subroutine for concatenating two text strings. The awk program concatenates strings that are placed next to each other without intervening operators.

conditional   A programming language construct that causes a statement (or statements) to be executed only if a certain condition is true. Typical conditionals are if and case statements.

conditional compilation   The ability to selectively compile parts of a program source file, based on certain logical conditions. The C language has a conditional compilation feature that, on UNIX systems, is implemented by the C preprocessor. Sections of code bracketed by #if (or #ifdef) and #endif are either compiled or ignored, based on the expression supplied with the #if statement. *See also* #if; #ifdef; C preprocessor.

conditional operator   *See* operator, conditional.

configuration   A particular assemblage of hardware or software components. For example, one common hardware configuration for a certain brand of computer might include a certain CPU, two disk drives, and nine communication lines. One of the most important duties of a UNIX system administrator is to manage the configurations of the system hardware and software. During the *system generation* process the configuration of the UNIX kernel is adjusted to match the hardware environment. This process entails adding and deleting device drivers so that the kernel contains the correct set. Another aspect of configuring a UNIX system is adjusting its variable parameters to match expected usage.

configure   To select compatible computer hardware components, or to adapt a software system (such as UNIX) to a particular assembly of hardware. *See also* configuration.

console   Main terminal, for use by the system manager or super-user. On midsize and large UNIX systems the console is usually a printing terminal, so that there is a paper record of error messages, crashes, and so on. The conventional name for the character special file that provides access to the console is '/dev/console'.

constant   A data element in a program whose value does not change. The Pascal language contains symbolic constants, which means that you can assign a name to a value (like naming a variable) but then that name represents a constant. The C language has two similar facilities; you can define a macro whose value is a constant, or you can use enumeration variables.

constant expression   An expression whose elements are all constants; thus, the result of the expression is a constant.

constant expression, restricted   A C language constant expression that is used in a C preprocessor directive. To relieve the preprocessor of the burden of understanding C, restricted constant expressions cannot use the sizeof operator, enumeration constants, or type casts.

context address   In the standard UNIX text editors, a specification of a location in a text file by mentioning the text pattern that appears at that location. For example, the ed or ex editor command /red/,/blue/p prints a region of the file, from the first following line that contains the text *red* to the line after that that contains the text *blue*. *See also* context search.

context search   A search for a location in a text file based on a text pattern. In the UNIX system a context search may be performed within an editor or by using the grep command. *See also* context address; grep.

contiguous   Pertaining to things that are lying next to each other, such as items in a list that are adjacent. Many simple operating systems employ a contiguous filesystem, which means that each file is located in a contiguous series of blocks on the disk. The UNIX system does not use a contiguous filesystem; rather, the blocks in each file are scattered throughout the disk. *See also* fragmentation.

continue statement   A flow-of-control statement in many languages that causes the next iteration of a loop to begin, skipping any remaining statements in the body of the loop. In the Bourne shell, a statement that starts the next iteration of the enclosing while, for, or until statement. In the C shell, a statement that otarto the next iteration of the enclosing while or foreach statement. In the C language, a statement that starts the next iteration of the enclosing do, while, or for statement.

control character   A nongraphic character that has been assigned a special meaning, such as the ASCII Ctrl-M character, which signifies the carriage return operation. Control characters are embedded in text to specify various operations, such as cursor movement or printing format. A control character is typed at a terminal by simultaneously depressing the control key (CTRL) and another key. The UNIX tty handler interprets many control characters as requests for the system to perform a function. For example, if you strike Ctrl-D (the end-of-file character) while a program is reading from the terminal, the kernel notifies that program that it has reached the end of its input.

control code   *See* escape sequence.

<Control-D>   *See* end of file character.

controller   A hardware interface that allows devices such as disks, tapes, and communications equipment to be attached to a computer.

cooked mode   An input mode of the UNIX teletype handler, in which the input is made available to programs one line at a time, not one character at a time. In cooked mode it is possible for a program to read a single character at a time, but no input is available to the program until after the entire line has been typed, including the carriage return. This is why UNIX shell commands do not take effect until you hit the return key; the shell can not even see them until after you strike return. cooked is the usual mode of the teletype handler. The term is, in some sense, the opposite of the word *raw*, which is the term used for the opposite condition—single character input. An intermediate input mode is Berkeley's cbreak mode. *See also* raw mode; cbreak mode.

core   A term for the main memory of a computer. The term, while widely used, is a holdover from the time when core memory technology was dominant. *See also* core memory.

core dump   Output of all values in a process' memory following a program failure. The kernel performs the core dump when certain signals arrive, or certain situations occur. For example, if a program consumes too much stack space, attempts to divide by zero, or attempts to access memory outside of its allocated region, the kernel will perform a core dump. In the UNIX system this information is put into a file named 'core' in the program's working directory, and then the system prints a brief message such as *Memory fault: core dumped*. When a core dump occurs, notify the system management so that the software can be repaired. Core dumps can be analyzed by programmers to deduce the cause of the failure using debuggers. The UNIX system has a variety of debuggers, including adb, sdb, and dbx. Nonprogrammers who cause a program to dump core should, in the absence of expert advice, simply remove the file named 'core' and avoid whatever action led to the core dump. Never use the name 'core' for your own files, because the system may overwrite it with a core dump, should one occur.

core memory   An obsolete memory technology, based on small magnets whose magnetic field orientation coded the individual bit values.

cpio   A UNIX program that can collect a group of files into a single file, usually so that they can be placed on a tape. Individual files can be extracted from a cpio format archive. cpio can also be used to copy filesystem subtrees from one place to another, and for making backups. The directory information at the head of some cpio archives is in binary format, which makes it difficult to transport cpio tapes between dissimilar computer systems. The word *cpio* comes from the phrase *copy in/out*. *See also* magnetic tape; tar.

cpio archive   A tape or file in the cpio format. *See also* cpio.

cpio tape   A tape in the cpio format. *See also* cpio.

CPP   The C Preprocessor. *See* C preprocessor.

C preprocessor   A component of the UNIX C compiler. In the UNIX system the C preprocessor is a separate program that performs the first stage processing in a compilation. The role of the C preprocessor is to provide a simple macro facility, to manage conditional compilation, and to include other files into the text of a program being compiled. Directives in a C program that apply to the C preprocessor start with a # character. Although all C compilers must provide the functionality of the UNIX C preprocessor, it need not be a separate program, as in the UNIX system. *See also* macro; conditional compilation; file inclusion.

CPU (central processing unit)   The control, arithmetic, and logical unit of a computer. The speed of the CPU is one of the major elements that determines the overall speed of a computer system. Many modern CPUs work with either 16 or 32 bits at once.

<CR>   *See* carriage return.

crash

An unexpected interruption of computer service, usually due to a serious hardware or software malfunction.

To unexpectedly fail. The term is rarely applied to minor failures; instead, it is usually reserved for serious failures. Both hardware and software can crash.

cron   A UNIX daemon that performs the chores listed in (at the times specified in) '/usr/lib/crontab'.

crontab   The '/usr/lib/crontab' file that specifies when periodic tasks should be performed.

cross-compiler   Software for compiling a program on one system for execution on a different system. UNIX systems often run cross-compilers. This allows programmers to take advantage of UNIX's powerful features while developing software for another system. UNIX systems are often used to develop software for robots, industrial computers and other computers that do not have their own development systems. UNIX systems are also sometimes used to develop software for powerful supercomputers.

CRT   An acronym for cathode ray tube, which is the principal element of most display terminals and televisions.

A computer terminal consisting of a CRT display and a keyboard. Also called a *video display terminal* (VDT).

C shell   A shell created by William Joy at the University of California at Berkeley. The syntax of the C Shell is borrowed both from the C programming language and from the primeval Version 6 UNIX shell. The C shell is admired for is powerful features for interactive command entry, such as its history mechanism and job control. It is less widely used than the Bourne shell for writing command scripts because it is not available on all UNIX systems.

curly brace   *See* brace.

current directory   *See* directory, current.

current subtree   Subtree whose root is the current directory. The current subtree consists of the current directory, all its subdirectories and files, their subdirectories and files, and so on.

curses   A C subroutine library to allow programs to easily display output at specific positions on the screen of a cathode-ray tube (CRT). The curses subroutine library uses the termcap terminal capabilities database. curses and termcap were originally developed for the vi text editor.

cursor   Special symbol on a display terminal that indicates the position where the next character will appear. The cursor, usually a small box or underline, may be blinking.

D

daemon   A program that runs unattended to perform a standard service. Some daemons are triggered automatically to perform their task; others operate periodically. One example is the UNIX system's cron daemon, which periodically performs the tasks listed in the '/usr/lib/crontab' file. Many standard dictionaries accept the spelling *demon*; UNIX gurus do not.

data   Basic elements of information that can be processed or produced by a computer.

database   A software system optimized for storing and retrieving information. The UNIX system does not have a standard database system, but there are numerous database systems that run on UNIX systems. (Also written as two words.)

data processing   Using machines (usually computers) to manipulate information. The term *data processing* is often used to connote computer-based business activity.

data region   One of the regions in a UNIX binary executable file. The data region contains all the initialized data in a program. The size of a binary executable file's data region is printed by the size program. *See also* text region; BSS region.

data structure   A collection of data elements that, taken together, describes an entity. A data structure, which exists in a process, is roughly analogous to a record, which exists in a data file. The separate elements in a data structure may have different types, and each element has its own name. Contrast with an *array*, whose elements are all of the same type, and whose elements are selected by an index expression (not by name). It is common to have arrays of data structure. The C language data type used to define a data structure is called struct. Several of the more important data structures in the UNIX kernel are the process table, the user table, the bdevsw table, and the cdevsw table. The following is a C language declaration of a data structure that might be used to describe a baseball player.

```
struct player {
    char name[30];
    int runs, hits, errors, atbats;
    double salary;
    };
```

In this data structure, there is a 30-character string to hold the player's name, integer variables to store several key statistics, and a floating-point variable to store the salary. *See also* array; record; bdevsw; cdevsw; user table; and process table.

dbx   A symbolic debugger available on Berkeley UNIX systems.

debug   To find and fix errors, usually in a program or command script.

debugger   A program that is designed to help programmers to find errors (bugs) in their programs. Typical debuggers let you examine memory, examine the values of a program's variables, and execute a program in a controlled manner. The UNIX system has several debuggers. adb is the most universal UNIX debugger, but it is relatively low level. Berkeley systems contain dbx, and System 5 contains sdb, both of which are regarded as higher-level debuggers.

decimal   The base ten number system, also called the *base ten radix* or *decimal radix.*

decimal constant   An constant written using the base ten radix. In C, such constants must start with one of the digits one through nine, because numeric constants that start with a zero are presumed to be octal or hexadecimal.

declaration

A specification of the type and name of a variable to be used in a program. Declarations are not necessary in shell programs because the shell creates variables dynamically as necessary, and because all shell variables are one type: text.

In C, a statement that specifies the names and attributes of variables, types, or functions. The purpose of a declaration is to provide enough information about an object so that the C compiler can generate code that relates to that object. A *type* declaration specifies the type's characteristics so that variables of that type can be declared. A *variable* declaration specifies the variable's name and type so that the compiler can generate code for expressions involving that variable. A *function* declaration specifies the function's result and parameter types, so that the compiler can correctly generate code to call that function. The missing aspect of a declaration is setting aside storage for a variable or for a function body—that is, done in a C definition. The C language has a novel syntax for declarations. Its syntax is extremely flexible and powerful, but difficult to learn. The essence of understanding a C declaration is to read it from the inside out. For example, the declaration

```
float (*x())[];
```

states that x is a function (the ( )s) returning a pointer to (the *) an array of (the []) floating-point numbers. When you are trying to read a C declaration, the symbol () (with nothing inside) is pronounced *function returning*, an * is pronounced *pointer to*, and [] is pronounced *array of*. Start with the variable name, and remember that the symbols on the right (( ) and []) have higher precedence than do the symbols appearing to the left (*). Parentheses alter the usual precedence, and they should similarly alter the order in which you read the declaration. *See* definition.

declarator   In C, the object whose characteristics are specified in a declaration or definition. For example, in the declaration int i;, the variable i is the declarator.

default

A value or action that will be used in the absence of an explicitly specified alternative. For example, the default output file for the UNIX C compiler is 'a.out'. If the –o file command line specification is used, then output will instead be sent to the specified file.

To revert to a predetermined action.

#define   A C language directive that defines a macro. On UNIX systems, this directive is executed by the C preprocessor.

defined (preprocessor operator)   A C language operator that can be used in restricted constant expressions. If the operand of defined has been previously defined, then the result is true, otherwise the result is false. *See also* #if.

definition   In C, a declaration of a variable that sets aside space for that variable and that may specify the initial value of the variable. Or (also in C), a declaration of a function that specifies the function body. C definitions go farther than declarations because they fully specify a function or variable, to the point where space can be reserved for the defined item. *See also* declaration.

delete   To remove something, often a file, a directory, or a component of a file, such as a word, a line, or a record. The ed and ex text editors use the d command to perform deletions, while the the vi text editor has several deletion commands, including the x command to delete a single character, and the d operator to delete a text object. The UNIX command to delete a file is rm. The technical term for deleting a UNIX file is unlinking, because the removal actually removes a link from a directory entry to an i-node. The UNIX system call for removing a link is unlink.

delimiter   A special symbol that is used to separate one thing from another. For example, in the C language comments are delimited by /* and */ symbols. In the shells, the delimiter for words is *white space*, which is spaces or tabs. *See also* field separator.

demand paged   A computer memory management system that reads in memory pages from disk when they are needed. *See also* paging.

dereference   To access the value pointed to by an address expression. The C language dereference operator is the *. C programmers must be careful not to confuse the * dereference operator, with the * multiplication operator. The main visual difference is that the dereference operator is a prefix unary operator, while the multiplication operator is a binary operator. Thus in the expression 50 * *p the first asterisk (a binary operator) indicates multiplication, while the second asterisk (unary prefix) indicates an access to the value stored at the address stored in the pointer named p. *See also* indirection.

descriptor, file   *See* file descriptor.

device   *See* peripheral device; device file; special file.

device, block   *See* block device.

device, character   *See* character device.

device dependent   A software system that is designed to operate with a specific input or output device. *See also* device independent.

device driver

Software that enables an operating system to transmit data between the computer and a peripheral device. Selecting an appropriate group of device drivers is one of the main chores during UNIX system generation. Within the UNIX kernel, device drivers are accessed via the cdevsw and bdevsw device driver tables. From UNIX applications programs, device drivers are accessed via (character and block) special files.

Applications software that adapts a software package to the needs of a particular I/O device. For example, the termcap subroutine package contains drivers that allow programs to access the major features of most video terminals. Many word processors and text formatters access drivers so that they can access printer features.

device file   A file in the UNIX filesystem that is used to access an I/O device. The more formal term is special device file. There are two types, character and block. *See also* special file; character special file; block special file.

device independent   Relating to a software system that is designed to work with a range of hardware I/O devices. For

43

example, a text formatter such as `ditroff`, which is designed to output to any capable printer, is said to be device independent. The original `troff`, which was designed to output one specific printer, is said to be device dependent. Device independent software usually relies on a device driver to adapt to a particular device.

Dhrystone

A standard figure of merit that indicates aspects of a system's performance other than its floating-point performance. The term is a dry spoof on the term *Whetstone*, which is a floating-point benchmark.

A benchmark program that measures the Dhrystone performance of a system.

diagnostic

An error message produced by a program. Some diagnostics indicate user errors, others indicate program failures, or other system problems, such as running out of temporary storage space.

Software provided by manufacturers to help locate errors in their equipment.

dial-up terminal A terminal that is connected to a computer via the public telephone network. Access to the public telephone network is through a modem. Terminals that are not connected via the public telephone system are directly connected. *See also* modem; direct connection.

dialogue A conversation between the user and the UNIX system. In the usual UNIX system dialogue the shell displays a prompt; the user then enters a command followed by a carriage return, the command is executed, and the shell then displays another prompt. You can also have a dialogue with other interactive parts of the system, such as the *vi* text editor.

direct connection Hardwired connection between devices and/or computers. A direct connection does not go through a public telephone system, although many large installations have local switches that enable a terminal to be connected to any computer in the installation. A direct connection between a terminal and the UNIX system is in contrast to a dial-up connection. *See also* dial-up terminal.

direct-connect modem   A modem that is electrically connected to the telephone system, in contrast to an acoustic coupler. Direct connect modems can operate at higher speeds than acoustic couplers, and they can be operated without manual intervention by programs such as uucp. *See also* modem; acoustic coupler.

direct memory access (DMA)   A hardware capability of many peripheral devices that allows them to transfer data to/from memory without direct CPU supervision. To do this, the peripheral requests access to memory and then manages each memory transfer itself. Peripherals that lack DMA capability must have their data transferred to/from memory by the host CPU, a technique that generally has lower performance. Peripherals that require very high I/O bandwidth, such as disks and tapes, often have DMA circuitry.

directory   A group of files in the UNIX filesystem; a group of files listed in a directory file. Directories are used to organize and structure the filesystem. Without the organization provided by the UNIX system's hierarchical directory system, it would be very difficult to manage the thousands of files that exist in typical UNIX system installations. The ls command is used to list the files in a directory. When a user logs onto the system, that person is in the home directory. The user can move to another directory by using the cd command or can print the name of the current directory by using the pwd command. *See also* directory file; directory, .; directory, ..; directory, current; directory access mode; directory, parent; directory, root; directory, home.

directory, . (dot)   In the UNIX system the name . (pronounced *dot*) is a synonym for the name of the current directory. Any program that wants to access the current directory can open the file named .. Users sometimes enter a dot as part of a file specification, if they want to state clearly that the desired file is in the current directory. For example, to run a program named test in the current directory (instead of the program by the same name

45

that is located elsewhere), one would enter the command ./test. The . entry is present in all UNIX directories. It is placed there when the kernel creates a directory, and it cannot be removed by the rm command. If you use the -i (show i-node number) option of the ls command, you can see that the name . in the current directory is a link to the same i-node as the directory's name in the parent directory.

```
$ pwd
/usr1/kc
$ ls -i . /usr1/kc
  854 .
  854 /usr1/kc
$ _
```

See also directory, current; directory, ..; directory; . (dot);

directory, .. (dot dot)   In the UNIX system the name .. (pronounced *dot dot*) is the generic name for the parent directory of the current directory. Users often use the name .. to create pathnames that ascend the filesystem. For example, the pathname '../../bin' starts in the current directory, ascends to its parent, ascends further to its parent's parent, and then descends to the 'bin' directory. Every directory contains an entry named .., and it cannot be removed by the rm command. The -i (show i-node number) option of the ls program can show you that the name .. in the current directory is a link to the same i-node as the parent directory.

```
$ pwd
/usr1/kc
$ ls -i .. /usr1
  301 ..
  301 /usr1
$ _
```

See also directory, parent; directory, .; directory; .. (dot dot).

directory access mode   The permissions that govern access to a directory. A directory, like other files, has three operations (reading, writing, and executing) that can be allowed or denied to three classes of users (the file's owner, members of the file's group, and others). For a directory, read privilege means that a user's program can open the directory for reading, to discover what files are in the directory. For a directory, write privilege means that a process can create or remove files in that directory. However, processes are never allowed to open a directory and write directly into it; the only way for a process to alter a directory file is to create or delete files in that directory. Only the kernel writes into directory files. For a directory, the execute privilege means that the directory can be used as part of a pathname. You cannot cd to a directory whose execute privilege is denied, nor can you access any file in that directory. *See also* file access mode; write permission.

directory, current   Your current location in the UNIX filesystem. Also called the working directory. Files in the current directory are directly accessible without specifying a full pathname. At all times in a user's interactions with the UNIX system there is a current directory. The name of the current directory can be printed using the pwd command. A user can move to another directory, which then becomes the current directory, by using the cd command. *See also* directory, .; directory, ..; cd; pwd.

directory file   A fundamental UNIX file type that contains a list of files and i-node numbers. Although UNIX programs are able to read directory files, they cannot directly write into a directory file. However, a UNIX program can ask the UNIX kernel to add or delete entries in a directory file using various UNIX system calls. Each directory file specifies the contents of a particular UNIX directory.

directory, home   The directory into which a user is placed at the immediate conclusion of the login process, the root directory of an individual's personal subtree in the UNIX filesystem, and the default destination for the command cd. The home directory of each user is catalogued in the '/etc/passwd' file.

directory, parent   The directory above the current one in the UNIX filesystem hierarchy. In the parent directory, the current directory appears as a subdirectory. The parent directory has the same i-node number as the .. entry in the current directory. *See also* directory, ...

directory, root   Every UNIX filesystem has a root directory. It is the directory from which all other directories on that filesystem arise, either directly or indirectly. However, what most UNIX users mean when they use the term *root directory* is the root directory of the root filesystem, which is the directory from which all other directories on a UNIX system arise, either directly or indirectly. The term *root directory* is necessary because the root directory is the only directory in the system that does not have a given name. Other directories are named in their parent directory. For example, the '/usr/bin' directory has the name *bin* because that name appears in '/usr', the parent directory of '/usr/bin'. Because the root directory doesn't have a parent, it doesn't have a given name. Absolute pathnames start in the root directory (of the root filesystem).

directory stack   A feature of the C shell that makes it easy to visit one (or more) directories and then return to your original location. The C shell contains the pushd command that pushes the name of the current directory onto the stack and then moves to the specified directory. The popd command does the opposite; it takes the top directory name off of the stack and returns to that location. A related C shell command is dirs, which displays the stack.

disk   The medium used in a disk drive. Disks are typically thin platters covered with a magnetic or optical material. Disks are classified as rigid (also called *fixed* or *hard*) or flexible (often called *floppies* or *diskettes*) according to the stiffness of the platter. Permanently sealed hard disks are usually called Winchester disks. Hard disks are available in two varieties: removable (from the disk drive) and nonremovable. Floppy diskettes are almost always removable. Hard disks usually have a greater storage capacity and operate more rapidly than floppy disks.

disk controller   An electrical circuit, usually housed on a plug-in circuit board, that acts as an interface between a disk drive and a computer system. The disk controller accepts software commands from the computer and controls the disk drive via. electrical signals, enabling transfer of data to/from the disk drive.

disk drive   Hardware device that uses rotating magnetic or optical media (disks) to store information; a type of mass storage device.

The disk drive is the electromechanical part of a disk subsystem. Disk drives are usually connected via a cable to a disk controller.

disk file   Named collection of information residing on a mass storage device. Disk files are said to be nonvolatile because they are retained even when operating power is removed from the mass storage device.

diskless node   A networked computer, usually a workstation, that does not have its own disk. Instead it relies on the disk of another computer, which it accesses via a local area network. *See also* NFS.

display terminal   Computer terminal that uses a CRT as its output device.

ditroff   The modern, device independent version of troff. *See* troff.

DMA   *See* direct memory access.

document

Textual information, either on paper on in a text file. In lay usage, any printed information is a document. However, in technical usage, a document usually refers to descriptions of equipment, software, procedures, and other technical information.

To write documentation.

documentation   Documents describing the design, installation, operation, or repair of hardware or software.

Documenter's Workbench   A set of programs that are an enhancement of the original UNIX typesetting software. They consist of the new version of troff, called ditroff, plus additional preprocessors, and other software relating to typesetting.

do statement   A C language iterative statement that repeatedly executes a statement (or group of statements) while a given condition is satisfied. The difference between a do and while is that in a do loop the body of the loop is executed first, and then the continuation condition is tested, whereas in a while loop the continuation test comes first. The body of a do loop is always executed at least once (each time the statement is encountered), whereas the body of a while loop won't be executed if its condition is initially false. *See also* while statement.

double indirect block   A part of the UNIX system's data structures for accessing files. A double indirect block is a block on a disk that contains the addresses of a group of indirect blocks, which in turn contain the addresses of the blocks of a file. A pointer in a file's i-node indicates the location of a file's first indirect block. If more indirect blocks are needed, their addresses are contained in a double indirect block. Only needed for very large files. *See also* indirect block; triple indirect block.

double type   A C language data type that holds a real (floating-point) number. C's other real number data type is float, which usually takes half as much storage space. *See also* float type.

driver   *See* device driver.

dump

A record of the state of a program at the time of a failure. *See* core dump.

To create a core dump.

To display, in an unambiguous form, the values in a file. The UNIX system contains the od program to produce displays in octal (the default), decimal, hexadecimal, or ASCII notation of the contents of a file. The UNIX system also contains more sophisticated programs, such as adb, sdb, and dbx, for examining files.

A type of backup, in which files are copied to tape by the dump program. Dumps are created on a regular basis, often daily, at most UNIX installations.

A program used to backup a filesystem.

To create a backup, using the dump program.

An informal term for moving or copying data, usually implying a large quantity of data.

dump, core   *See* core dump.

dump, full   A backup in which all files are copied to tape by the dump program.

dump, incremental   A backup in which files modified after a certain time are copied to tape by the dump program.

duplex, full   *See* full duplex.

duplex, half   *See* half duplex.

dynamic memory   A technique for building memory circuits based on using capacitance to store a charge. Presence of a charge is taken as one state; absence of the charge is the opposite state. Because charge slowly drains away from all capacitors, dynamic memory must be periodically refreshed, which means that all charged elements are brought back to a fully charged state. The periodic refresh requirement somewhat complicates the design of dynamic memory circuitry. Dynamic memory is the densest and least expensive (per bit of storage) memory technology, but it is not the highest-performance technology, and it loses its information when the power is removed. Dynamic memory is used for the main memory of all personal computers, and most other computers. *See also* static memory; read-only memory; programmable read-only memory; ultraviolet erasable programmable read-only memory.

EBCDIC Extended binary-coded decimal interchange code. An eight-bit character coding system used primarily on IBM (and compatible) mainframe computers. The UNIX system is available on such computers, although UNIX has a strong ASCII heritage. *Pronounced* ehb-sih-dick. *See also* ASCII; character set.

echo

A characteristic of the UNIX tty handler relating to the UNIX system's repetition of the user's typed input. The characters typed by a user are normally sent to the UNIX system and then returned so that they appear on the terminal. Echoing is occasionally turned off (for instance, during password entry).

To reproduce input, as done by the UNIX tty handler to most typed input, or by the echo command to its command-line arguments.

A UNIX command that echos its command-line arguments.

ed ed is the original UNIX system text editor. Although not widely used in modern UNIX systems, ed is historically important for giving a flavor and a direction to many other programs. The line editing persona of the ex/vi editor is derived form ed, as is the underlying pattern matching behavior of many other UNIX programs, including lex, awk, sed, and grep. Many early UNIX programs adopted an ed-like user interface, including the mail program and the adb debugger. *See also* editor, line; editor, visual; editor, text; ex.

edit To change or alter information. Often used in reference to changing the text in a text file by using a text editor such as vi.

edit buffer　　The name for the storage area used by an editor such as ed or vi while you are editing a file. During an editing session, a copy of the original file (plus any changes that you have made) is kept in the edit buffer. At the end of a successful editing session the edit buffer should be copied to a disk file, using the editor's write command. If the editor unexpectedly dies, any changes made to the edit buffer (since the last save) will be lost.

editor　　*See* editor, text.

editor, line　　A text editor that creates and modifies files by displaying and operating on one line at a time, or on a group of lines, to perform each change. Typical line editor commands allow you to print, delete, add, copy, or move lines of text. There are also commands to make individual changes on a line, such as changing the spelling of a word. Line editors are powerful because they can easily make a given change on many lines of a file. However, they are considered to be harder to use and less intuitive than visual editors. The original UNIX line editor was ed, although the most commonly used line editor on modern systems is ex. *See also* ed; ex; editor, text; editor, visual.

editor script　　A command script that is designed to control the operation of a text editor to automatically make some alteration to a text file. Early UNIX system editor scripts were designed for the ed editor; on modern systems editor scripts are primarily written for the sed editor, although scripts for ed or ex are occasionally developed.

editor, text　　A general-purpose program used to prepare and manipulate text files. A text editor enables users to enter and modify text. Most editors accept commands to locate specific lines or words in the text and commands to add, delete, change, and print lines in the text. Unlike a word processor, a text editor is not very concerned with the appearance of the text. A text editor does not manage margins, headers, footnotes, and so forth, although it does let you enter format control codes to control those features. The standard UNIX text editor is vi, although many other text editors are available. *See also* word processor; text formatter.

53

editor, visual   A text editor that maintains a representation of a region of a file on the screen of the terminal. This makes the screen a window into the file during the editing session. *See also* vi; emacs.

effective group id   The group id number that is used to help determine access rights to a file, when access is not allowed as a result of user id rights. When a set group id program is executing, the effective group id is the group associated with the executable file; otherwise, it is the group id affiliation of the user. *See also* group id; group id number.

effective id   The group or user id number that is used to determine file access rights. When a set user (or group) id program is running, it is that executable file's user (or group) id affiliation that is used; otherwise it is the user's user (or group) id affiliation that is used. *See also* user id number.

effective user id   The user id number that is used to help determine access rights to a file. When a set user id program is executing, the effective user id is the owner of the executable file; otherwise, it is the user id affiliation of the user. *See also* user id; user id number.

elapsed time   *See* execution time.

electronic mail   Method of transmitting information (memos, messages, letters, etc.) to other users of a computer system or to users on other systems.

em   A unit of typographic measure, approximately equal to the width of a capital letter *M* in the current font and point size. Horizontal distances are often specified in ems.

emacs   Programmable text editor first developed at MIT by Richard Stallman. emacs is not a standard part of either System V or Berkeley UNIX, but versions of emacs are available for all UNIX systems. *See also* visual editor.

embedded assignment   An assignment expression placed somewhere that a person accustomed to Pascal, Algol, or Fortran would not expect. Embedded assignments are possible in C, because assignment is performed by an operator and is allowed in any expression, unlike most other languages where assignment is a type of statement. In C, code similar to the following is very common. This particular fragment is a while loop whose test expression reads in a character, assigns that character to the variable ch, compares the character to the constant EOF, and then performs the body of the loop if ch and EOF are different.

```
while((ch = getchar()) != EOF) {
    . . .
}
```

The equivalent operation written without using embedded assignment is the following.

```
ch = getchar();
while(ch != EOF) {
    . . .
    ch = getchar();
}
```

em dash   A dash that is one em wide, which is wider than a hyphen or minus sign. The troff text formatter makes em dashes only three quarters of an em long.

emulate   For one device to simulate the operation of another.

emulation

Simulation of a device or process.

Many third-party suppliers of hardware for UNIX computers sell interfaces that emulate the capabilities of the manufacturer's interfaces. Emulations are never exactly the same; before buying such hardware you should ascertain from independent sources that the emulation will work reliably with your version of UNIX software.

emulator, terminal   A program (often on a micro, but also in other situations, such as in a window on a graphic workstation) that simulates the operation of a particular model of terminal. For example, there are many programs on personal computers that emulate the DEC VT100 terminal.

en   A typographic unit of measure, equal to one half of an em (one-half of the width of a capital *M* in the current font and point size). Often used in specifying horizontal layout. In nroff, which is designed to output to typical impact printers, an en represents the same width as an em, which is the width of a typical character.

encrypt   To convert a file to a form that cannot be readily understood. *See also* encryption.

encryption   Converting a file (or other information, such as a login password) into a form that cannot be readily understood, to protect the privacy of the information. The UNIX system contains the crypt program to encrypt and decrypt files. Encryption is a much stronger guarantee of privacy than the UNIX system's file access system.

end of file (eof)

The point past which further information cannot be acquired from a file. Attempting to read data past the end of a file will return a standard error condition.

A special mark on a magnetic tape, signifying the end of a file. Tape-handling software recognizes EOF marks. *See also* end-of-tape mark.

end-of-file character   Control-D is the standard UNIX system end-of-file (EOF) character. When a process is reading data from the terminal, you can strike the end-of-file character to signal the end of the input. The process will not literally acquire the end-of-file character (the Control-D); rather, it will receive an indication from the system that the end has been reached. Since the shell normally stops processing when it encounters EOF, one way to log off the UNIX system is to strike Control-D in response to a shell prompt.

end-of-tape mark   A mark signifying the end of all data on a magnetic tape. Often it is two consecutive end of file marks.

enter key   *See* carriage return.

enter   To input information. For example, during the login procedure the UNIX system prompts you to enter (type in) your login
name and password.

enum   The C language keyword that is used to define an enumeration.

enumeration type   A C language data type that allows you to
define a set of named integer constants and to declare variables of
that type. This is an alternative to using C macros to name constant values.

environment   Characteristics of a user's account, such as the
home directory, the group affiliation, and the environment variables.

environment variables   Shell variables that are exported, so that
their values can be used by every command executed by the shell.
$TERM, $HOME, and $PS1 are common environment variables. The
Bourne shell's export command is used to mark a variable so that
it is exported each time it runs a command. The C shell has three
commands for manipulating environment variables: setenv to mark
a variable for export, unsetenv to remove a variable from the environment, and printenv to print the variables in the environment.
See also export.

EOF character   *See* end of file character.

EOT mark   *See* end of tape mark.

eqn   A troff preprocessor that makes it easier to typeset mathematical equations. *See also* troff.

erase character   The erase character erases previously typed
characters on the current terminal input line, one at a time. On
many systems it is assigned initially to the sharp key (#) or to the
backspace key. It can be reassigned to another key using the
stty command. Such character reassignment stty commands are
often placed in users '.login' or '.profile' login script. During the
login process (entering your login name and password) the erase

character is usually set to the systemwide default; thus, during this procedure you must erase characters using that key. The reassignment to the key of your choice does not occur until your login shell starts to execute and encounters a key reassignment stty command in your login script. *See also* interrupt character; kill character.

error message   Information about a problem that prevented successful completion of a program's or command's execution. *See* diagnostic.

escape

To temporarily exit from an interactive program. For example, most interactive UNIX programs let you temporarily escape from the program to enter shell commands by entering the ! command.

To disable the special meaning of shell (or other) metacharacters. In the shell this is done by preceding the metacharacter with a backslash or by enclosing the character inside quotes. *See also* backslash; metacharacter; quoting.

escape key

Usually labeled ESC on the keyboard. It is often used as a command key in interactive programs. In vi the escape key cancels text insert mode and returns to command mode. In emacs the escape key is a prefix that activates an alternate meaning for the following keystroke.

The escape key sends an ASCII ESC code, which is octal 033 (decimal 27). The same code is also sent as the first part of a multicharacter code by many of the function keys on most keyboards. *See also* escape character.

escape character

Literally, the ASCII character with octal code 033. It can be generated by striking the escape key or by striking Ctrl-[(control left bracket), and it is a part of many of the special codes that are used to control a terminal.

Any character in a character stream that is used to signal that some number of following characters are to be interpreted specially.

escape sequence   A sequence of codes that directs a terminal (or other device) to perform some operation, such as moving the cursor, clearing the screen, clearing a line, or starting/stopping a display mode such as underlining; or, a sequence of codes generated by a keyboard to identify a nonalphanumeric key, such as an arrow key or a function key. UNIX has two common subsystems that make it easy for programmers to manage the control codes for a wide variety of terminals: the terminfo system, which is used on System V, and the original termcap system, which is used on Berkeley systems. The name is derived from the fact that many escape sequences start with the escape character (033 octal). Also called a *control code.*

escape sequence, C   In a C string constant or character constant, a sequence of characters that represents another character. The reason for having escape sequences is to make it convenient to represent values that would otherwise be difficult to manage. C recognizes the following escape sequences.

\n	New line	\t	Carriage return
\b	Backspace	\f	Form feed
\'	Single quote	\"	Double quote
\v	Vertical tab	\t	Horizontal tab
\a	Bell (alert)	\\	Backslash
\ddd	Octal notation for an ASCII character	\xdd	Hexadecimal notation for ASCII character

See also hexadecimal character constant; octal character constant.

Ethernet   A baseband local area network developed by Xerox, Intel, and Digital Equipment Corporation. It consists of a cable and interface hardware connecting multiple computer systems. Only one system can use the cable at a time. Computer systems are free to use the network when they detect that other devices are not actively using the network. When (inevitable) collisions occur, the colliding devices must back off and try again (a few milliseconds) later.

Eunice   A version of UNIX that runs on VMS systems. Unlike most UNIX versions, which completely operate the computer hardware on which they are running, the Eunice system is a guest of VMS. The computer is running VMS; Eunice is simply a VMS task that creates a UNIX environment and allows most UNIX software to function.

ex   The line editing aspect of the vi text editor. *See also* vi; ed; editor, line.

exception   A hardware difficulty in a computer system that is typically caused by a software problem. For example, dividing by zero is likely to cause an exception. Exceptions are handled somewhat like hardware interrupts, but their cause is internal. Many computers contain instructions to cause an exception, such as the trap instruction, which unconditionally causes an exception, or the bounds check instruction, which causes an exception if a variable is out of range. UNIX programs that unintentionally generate an exception typically receive a signal, and they typically terminate (often with a core dump) if they have not made arrangements to handle that signal.

exec

A fundamental UNIX system call that overlays the current process with another. Following an exec, the original process is gone and another exists in its place. The pid of the new process is the same as the pid of the original. Use of the exec system call does not increase the number of processes, although it is often used in conjunction with the fork system call, which does increase the number of processes. When one process exec's another, the first does not exit, and a parent process waiting for the death of the first process will not be notified when the exec occurs. However, the parent will be notified when the second, or its successor, exits, because it has the same process id number as the original child process.

A built-in Bourne and C shell command that causes the current shell to be replaced by some other program.

To replace the current process with another.

executable file   A file that can be executed by the system. Some executable files contain binary machine instructions, while others are text files that contain shell scripts. Files may only be executed if the execute permission is set, using the chmod command, except when you explicitly direct a shell to execute the commands in a command script. The file command can determine the difference between binary executables and shell scripts. In UNIX the same command line syntax is used to run both types of executables.

execute   To run a program or routine. The UNIX system can execute binary files by loading them into memory and then executing them directly. To execute a shell script, the UNIX system must execute a shell (which is a binary executable), with its standard input attached to the script. In most versions of the UNIX system, the shell detects that certain executable files are scripts (not binary executables) and spawns a shell to interpret their contents. However in Berkeley UNIX systems, the kernel can directly spawn a shell to interpret a shell script. This Berkeley enhancement makes it possible for application programs to exec any executable (script or binary) using the exec system call; on other systems only binary executables can be exec'd by using the exec system call.

execute permission

For ordinary files, execute permission is a file access mode that allows a user to execute the file. The execute permission is set automatically by the compiler when it creates an executable file. User's can set the execute permission for their files using the chmod command. *See also* read permission; write permission; file access mode.

For directory files, execute permission is an access mode that allows a user to search those files in the course of resolving a pathname. You cannot cd to a directory unless you have execute permission for that directory. Similarly, you cannot include a directory in a pathname unless you have execute permission in that directory.

execution time   The time required by the computer to complete a given command or program. Execution times are displayed by the time command, or the C shell can be configured to display execution times whenever a process executes for more than a given length of time. The time command displays three numbers: the *elapsed* time, which indicates the length of time from start to finish; the *user* time, which indicates the length of time that the process executed its own instructions; and *system* time, which is the length of time that the system spent carrying out the process's requests.

execution   The computer's act of performing the instructions stored in a file. *See also* execute.

__exit   A C language interface that directly accesses the UNIX system exit system call.

exit

A fundamental UNIX system call that triggers the demise of a process. When a process exits, its parent may be notified, its files are closed, and all its resources (process table entry, space in core, etc.) are deallocated.

A C language subroutine. When a C program calls exit, or when the main routine in a C program returns, the exit subroutine is invoked. The role of the exit subroutine is to perform minor housekeeping, such as flushing I/O buffers, before actually invoking the _exit system call. exit reduces the number of active processes by one.

A built-in Bourne and C shell command that causes the shell to exit. If this command is given to your login shell, you will be logged out. If given to another shell, this will return you to a previous context.

For a UNIX process, to terminate its existence by calling the exit (or _exit) routine.

exit status   A numeric value provided on termination of a program to reflect its success or failure. A process can acquire the exit status of its offspring using the `wait` system call. In a Bourne shell script, the exit status of the previous command is stored in the $? built-in variable. In the C shell, the exit status of the previous command is stored in the `$status` variable.

export   To make a Bourne shell variable available to child processes, using the `export` command. *See* environment variable.

expression   A group of operators and operands that are grouped and organized according to the rules of a language and that represent a single value. Expressions are generally of two types: arithmetic and logical, although in many expressions the two types are combined. In many programming languages, such as C, expressions have both a type and a value. One unusual aspect of C is that assignment operations are considered expressions. As a consequence, one of the C statement types is an expression, but an expression statement need not be an assignment (as in most other languages). *See also* type.

extension   The part of a filename that follows a period, usually to identify the type of the file. For example, C source code files customarily have a *.c* extension, object code files customarily have a *.o* extension, and archive files customarily have a *.a* extension. Also called a suffix. *See also* basename.

external declaration   In C, a declaration or definition that appears outside a function. Externally declared variables (plus static local variables) exist for the lifetime of the program. All C functions are defined externally, and all of them exist for the lifetime of the program. *See also* declaration.

extern storage class   *See* storage class, extern.

fault An error. On particular computer systems there are often very specific erroneous conditions that are referred to as *faults*. For example, on many computers with memory management, accessing an address outside of a process' allocated space is often called a *memory fault*.

fault tolerant Able to recover from failure, usually by providing redundancy in the hardware and/or the software. Several fault tolerant versions of the UNIX system have been developed to service fault-intolerant applications such as on-line systems.

field

A portion of a command line, or a portion of each record (usually a line) in a file. Fields in a UNIX command line (usually called *words*) are customarily separated by spaces or tabs, as specified in the Bourne shell variable $IFS (internal field separators). In files, a field may be defined to span the same character positions on every line, or to be separated by a field separator character, such as a tab or a colon. *See also* field separator.

To manage an event, such as an interrupt or signal.

field separator A character, often a space, tab, colon, or comma, that separates consecutive fields in an input record. For example, the field separator in the '/etc/passwd' file is a colon. Also called a *delimiter*. The major UNIX utilities that work with fields are sort, awk, cut, and paste; you can specify the field separator for those programs using command line options. *See also* delimiter.

FIFO file (first in first out) In UNIX System V, a named permanent pipe. A FIFO allows two unrelated processes to exchange information using a pipe connection. Normal pipes work only with related processes. A FIFO is a file in the filesystem, but it is a special file, not an ordinary file. The system takes data from the process that is writing to the FIFO and transfers it to the process that is reading from the FIFO, almost as if the two processes had an ordinary pipe connection. FIFO files are created using the mknod command. Not all UNIX systems have FIFOs.

file A named entity in the UNIX filesystem. The UNIX system has the following file types.

Ordinary files, which are used to store data. The majority of files on a UNIX system are ordinary files. Created using the creat or open system call.

Directory files, which contain lists of files and their i-node numbers. They specify the contents of a directory. Created using the mkdir system call.

Character special files, which allow programs to access character I/O devices. Created using the mknod system call.

Block special files, which provide an interface to block I/O devices. They are usually mounted, so the kernel can access a filesystem stored on a block device. Created using the mknod system call.

FIFO files, which allow unrelated processes to have a pipelike connection. Created using the mknod system call. (System V only.)

Symbolic link files, which allow one file to be a pseudonym for another. Created using the symlink system call. (Berkeley only.)

Sockets, which are flexible communication endpoints. (Only UNIX-domain sockets appear in the UNIX filesystem.) UNIX domain sockets are associated with a particular filename using the bind system call. (Berkeley only.)

UNIX files are collected into groups called directories. *See also* special file; block special file; character special file; directory; directory file; FIFO; symbolic link; socket.

file access mode   The protection information for a UNIX file. In a shared computer system, access modes ensure a degree of privacy and safety for a user's files. In the UNIX system, files are owned by a user, and associated with one group of users. Files may be read, written, or executed by three classes of users: the file's owner, members of the file's group, or by others. For example, if a person belonging to the file's group tries to read a file whose group access permission is denied, the operation will not be allowed. Access modes are displayed in the first field of the long format ls listing, which is always ten characters long. The first field of the long format ls display is often called the *mode string*. Following the single character file type, the mode string contains three sets of three characters. The first set is *rwx*, if all owner permissions (*r*ead, *w*rite, and *e*xecute) are allowed. If a permission is denied, its corresponding letter is replaced by a dash. The second set of three characters is for the group permissions, and the final set is for other's permissions. Files with the set user id mode or set group id mode have a *s* in place of the owner or group execute privilege. Files with the save text (sticky) mode set have a *t* in place of the execute permissions for others. The access mode for a file, along with its ownership and group affiliation, is kept in the file's i-node. Thus a file with several names (links) has the same access mode for each of its names because all files have just one i-node. The chmod command is used to control file access modes. The umask Bourne and C shell commands let you control the default access modes for files that you create. (Also called *access privilege, access mode.*) *See also* file; save text mode; directory access mode; set user id; set group id.

file descriptor   A small number that is used by programs as a token for performing I/O. Whenever a program makes an I/O request, the file descriptor is passed to the operating system along with the I/O request to signify which I/O connection to use. On most UNIX systems a process can have approximately 20 I/O connections. By convention in the UNIX system, file descriptors 0, 1, and 2 are assigned to a process's standard input, standard output, and standard error output, respectively.

file inclusion   To insert one file into another, usually by placing a directive in the file that causes it to be inserted during a processing operation such as compilation, assembly, or text formatting. The C compiler uses the #include directive to specify file inclusion, which is performed on UNIX systems by the C preprocessor. The nroff/troff text formatter uses the .so command to specify file inclusion. *See also* C preprocessor; #include.

file locking   A capability of some operating systems that allows files to be locked while in use by one process, so that other processes will not be able to access them during that time. This makes it possible for multitasking database systems to operate reliably. *See also* record locking.

file mode   *See* file access mode.

filename   The name used to identify a particular file. Sometimes the term refers to the the full absolute pathname of a file, but more commonly it simply refers to the last component of the file's full pathname, which is the name as catalogued in the directory file. Within a directory, filenames are unique. Thus you cannot have two files named 'bin' in the '/usr' directory. However two files can have the same filename if they are stored in different directories, such as the directory '/bin' (a directory named 'bin' in the root directory) and '/usr/bin' (a directory named 'bin' in the '/usr' directory). Sometimes written as two words.

filename expansion   *See* filename generation.

filename generation   The procedure that the shell follows to expand command line words containing metacharacters (*, ?, and [] for Bourne, Korn and C shell, plus ˜ for the C shell and Korn shell) into a corresponding list of filenames. For example, in a directory containing the files 'x.doc', 'x.lst', and 'nm.doc' the shell's filename generation process will expand the word *.doc* into the list of files 'nm.doc' and 'x.doc', and it will expand the word *x.** into the list of file 'x.doc' and 'x.lst'. *See also* argument list generation.

file permissions   *See* file access mode.

file pointer

In the UNIX system, a variable that points toward one of the entries in the portable C I/O library FILE table. The portable C I/O

library's analog of a file descriptor. A variable whose type is FILE
* (pointer to FILE).

In general, a variable that indicates the current read/write location
in a file.

file server   A networked computer that can, via the network, act as
a filesystem for other computers on the network. This enables
computers with small disks, or computers without disks, to access
files on other systems. *See also* NFS, RFS.

filesystem   A collection of files (directory files, special files, ordinary files, etc.) and file management structures (i-nodes, the superblock) on a mass storage device. In the UNIX system the
filesystem is hierarchical; each directory can have subdirectories,
the subdirectories can have further subdirectories, and so on.
Small disks (less than 100 megabytes) sometimes contain a single
filesystem, but larger disks are usually partitioned into several
filesystems. Although details vary, most UNIX filesystems have the
following structure: a bootblock, a superblock, i-node blocks, and
then blocks for files. The bootblock and the superblock can be
more than one block long, and they are sometimes duplicated at
several locations to increase filesystem reliability.   The i-node
blocks typically consume a few percent of the space on a
filesystem. The great majority of space is actually allocated to the
storage of data. Each time a system boots, active filesystems are
examined by the fsck program to ensure that the structure of the
filesystem is intact. Filesystems are created by the mkfs command. Filesystem is sometimes written as two words. *See also*
file; filesystem layout; partition; i-node; bootblock; superblock.

filesystem layout   The location and size of each filesystem on a
disk. Large disks often contain more than one filesystem. There
are numerous reasons for partitioning a disk, such as making it
easier to back up selected filesystems, increasing reliability by seg-
regating filesystems, and keeping individual filesystems small
enough to be managed properly. Some UNIX systems contain
filesystem layout information in the header of each disk pack, so
that identical types of disks can have differing layouts. Other systems force all disks of a given type to have the same filesystem
layout. *See also* partition.

file type   Classification of a file according to its contents and function. The more fundamental type of a file is its UNIX classification. UNIX systems have ordinary files (information storage), directory files (groups of files), character special files, and block special files (access to I/O hardware). System V also contains FIFO files (pipe connections between unrelated processes), and Berkeley systems contain symbolic link files (a reference to another file) and socket files (communication endpoints). The type of each file is displayed symbolically in the first field of a long format ls listing using the following code.

–	Ordinary	d	Directory
c	Character special	b	Block special
s	Berkeley socket	l	Berkeley symbolic link
p	System V FIFO		

Each file's i-node contains its file type specification. Ordinary files are often categorized according to their usage. The file command intuits the contents of an ordinary file. *See also* file.

filter

A program that reads information from the standard input, (usually) modifies that information and then writes its results to the standard output. For example, the wc (word count) program reduces its standard input to a one line summary: its length in characters, words, and lines. Filters are an important part of the UNIX philosophy. Many applications have been developed using existing filters in novel configurations, using UNIX pipes.

To convert input data into output data.

filled text   A region of a document where all lines have about the same length. This can be done manually, by a text editor, or by a text formatter. For documents longer than a few pages, manually filling text is very time consuming and should be avoided. The UNIX system contains the nroff/troff system of text formatters, and the Berkeley system contains the fmt program, which can create filled text from more ragged text. If all lines are exactly the same length, the text is said to be fully justified. Text that is filled, but not justified, is said to have a ragged right (or occasionally a ragged left). The nroff/troff text formatters have the .nf command to disable subsequent filling, and the .fi command to enable filling of subsequent text.

firmware   Software that is permanently embedded in a computer, usually to perform power-on functions, or low-level access to I/O hardware. Firmware is usually stored in a ROM or EPROM circuit. The term emphasizes the fact that firmware is not hardware, but that it is harder to alter than software.

flag   *See* option.

floating point   A number system that can handle very large or small numbers and numbers with a fractional part. Floating-point numbers are stored with a fraction and an exponent. Arithmetic operations with floating-point numbers usually take longer than arithmetic operations with whole numbers. Floating-point numbers themselves are not always exact, but division with floating-point numbers is always performed as exactly as possible, unlike division of whole numbers, which discards the remainder. If a and b are floating-point variables with the values 1 and 2, then the expression a/b yields the result 0.5, but if they are whole number variables with the same values, then the same expression yields the answer 0.

float type   A C language data type that can hold a real number. The other C language real-number data type is double, which usually occupies twice the storage of a float datum. C programmers often create float variables (especially arrays of floats) to save space, but they do not decrease computation time because in C all real-number computations are done using double precision.

flow control   A mechanism, either hardware or software, for synchronizing the sender and receiver of data. Flow control is used to keep the sender from sending data too rapidly, thereby overwhelming the receiver and causing data loss. There are several simple software flow-control schemes for serial data links, including XOFF/XON and ENQ/ACK. The XOFF/XON system is usually used on serial links between computers and terminals. *See also* XOFF/XON.

flow of control   The path of execution in a program. In most programming languages, the flow of control is sequential, except when a flow of control statement is encountered. The following C code fragment contains an `if` flow-of-control statement. The flow of control starts at the top, going to the first two assignment statements. If the *if* condition is true, then flow of control goes to the three assignment statements in the *if* compound statement. Finally, flow of control visits the last statement, which calls the *drawvec* procedure. While *drawvec* is active, flow of control is dictated by its internal logic (not shown).

```
x = radius * cos(theta);
y = -radius * sin(theta);
if (x < y) {
    tmp = x;
    x = y;
    y = tmp;
}
drawvec(x,y);
```

flow-of-control statement   A command in a programming language, or a native machine instruction, that is capable of altering the normal sequential execution of instructions. The C language flow of control statements are `if`, `for`, `while`, `switch`, and `do`, plus its `goto` and procedure call statements. The Bourne shell's flow-of-control statements are `if`, `case`, `while`, `until`, `for`, and `case`, plus the `conditionals`. The C shell's flow of control statements are `foreach`, `goto`, `repeat`, `switch`, `while`, and `if`.

foo, foobar   Generic names. Often used whenever an identifier is required to complete an explanation, as in "the definition 'double foo();' states that *foo* is a procedure that returns a double."

for

In the Bourne shell, an iterative statement that executes a command list once for each parameter in a list of words, or once for each positional parameter (shell script argument) in the absence of an explicit word list.

In C, a flexible iterative statement. `for` statements are controlled by three expressions: an initialization expression, a continuation expression, and an increment expression. The statement governed by the `for` list is executed while the continuation expression is true (unless a `break` or `return` is executed). The initialization is performed before the first iteration, and the increment is performed at the conclusion of each iteration. *See also* iterative statements.

foreach   In the C shell, an iterative statement that executes a command list once for each word in a list.

foreground

A place where processes are said to be when they are being executed interactively. In the usual situation, the foreground process is either your login shell, or whatever process the login shell is waiting for. This definition applies repeatedly if you are running several layers of software. The UNIX kernel maintains just a single input stream for the terminal, and if multiple processes are all accessing that input stream, each will unpredictably get portions of the input. Such a situation is undesirable; hence the strong convention of having only one *active* foreground process (often plus several waiting foreground processes) at once.

To place a process in the foreground, usually using the Berkeley job control commands. *See also* background; job control.

foreground process   A process that is run interactively; a process that has first rights to access the terminal. There may be several active background commands, but under normal circumstances there will be just one active (and perhaps several inactive) foreground processes.

fork

One of the key UNIX system calls. Calling `fork` duplicates an existing process, thereby creating a new process. The two processes share open files and have the same values for all data elements. After the duplication, both processes proceed from the point at which `fork` was called (not from the beginning). The only difference between the two processes is that they have different pid numbers, and that in the parent the return value from the `fork` call is the pid of the child, while in the child the return value from the fork call is zero. One of the most common operations in the UNIX system, and one of particular importance to the shell, is a fork followed by an exec. This operation spins off a new process, while leaving the original process still running. When you run a program in the foreground, what actually happens is that the shell fork-execs the program, and then it calls wait to wait for the process's completion. The major difference when the shell runs a process in the background is that it omits the ensuing wait. *See also* exec.

For a UNIX process to split into two, by calling the fork system call.

formal parameters   The parameters of a procedure or function that appear in the function definition. Each time the procedure or function is invoked, the formal parameters take on the values of (or the references to, in a call by reference language) the actual arguments. Each procedure has only one set of formal parameters, although it can be called with many different actual arguments. *See also* actual arguments.

format

To place a standard pattern of structural and reference information onto a new disk pack (or sometimes onto a tape) so that it can subsequently be used. Often there are two different format operations: a low-level format that places rudimentary positioning information onto the media; and a high-level format that places system specific information, such as filesystem headers and empty i-node tables, onto the media.

To convert a text file that contains format codes and plain text (a marked-up document), into a more regular form, that is paginated, contains headers and footers, uniform line lengths, and so on. Most formatting is designed to send output to a particular brand of printer or typesetter. The standard UNIX text formatters are nroff and troff.

The appearance and/or layout of something, such as a document, a file, or a disk pack.

format code　A symbol (or group of symbols) that is placed into text files to specify the ultimate appearance of the file. For example, the `nroff/troff` format code to indicate italics is `\f2`, and the code to indicate extra vertical space in the output is `.sp` (which must appear alone on a line).

formatter

A program for placing format information onto a disk pack.

A program for converting a text file into a more regular form, usually with smoothed margins, headers and footers, and a uniform appearance. The UNIX system contains the programs `nroff` and `troff` for formatting text files. `nroff` is designed to output to an ordinary printer, while `troff` is designed to send its output to a typesetter, or to another printer with similar characteristics. *See* `troff`; `scribe`; TEX.

form feed　Movement to the top of the next page, usually on a printer or printing terminal.

form-feed character　An ASCII control character that makes most printers advance to the start of the next page. ASCII code 014 (octal) or 12 (decimal). Can be generated by striking Ctrl-L.

Fortran　The first high-level programming language. The name is derived from the phrase *formula translator*. Fortran remains widely used for heavily computational programs. There are several versions of Fortran available for UNIX systems, and several translators available that convert other languages into Fortran. The most widely used version is probably `f77`, which adheres to the 1977 Fortran standard.

fragmentation　The extent to which the blocks of a file are scattered throughout a filesystem. Over time, as the blocks in a filesystem are used and reused, the storage assigned to new files tends to become increasingly scattered throughout the disk. This can significantly slow access, particularly to larger files. Several utility programs exist that reassign the block usage of the filesystem, so that files are stored more contiguously. *See also* contiguous.

Franz Lisp   Berkeley's version of the Lisp programming language. *See* Lisp.

frontend   The part of a computer application that deals mostly with a user interface, unlike the backend, which manages data. The frontend of a compiler performs lexical and syntactical analysis. The frontend of a database management system manages the user dialogue. *See also* backend.

full dump   *See* dump, full.

full duplex   A characteristic of a communication system where information is capable of flowing in either direction at any time. Communication lines between UNIX and terminals are usually full duplex. *See also* half duplex.

function   A procedure that returns a value. In C, all procedures are functions, although by declaring a function to have the `void` type, a C programmer can explicitly state that a C procedure does not return a value. Unless declared otherwise, all C procedures have the `int` type. *See also* procedure.

function keys   Special keys that exist on many keyboards to be used in application specific ways. They keys are often numbered—for example, F1, or assigned generic labels that are useful to many applications, such as PgUp, Home, or End. Function keys generally produce a sequence of codes, often called an *escape sequence*, when they are pressed. Some UNIX applications are able to make use of function keys. For example, the `vi map` command lets you assign `vi` commands to your terminal's function keys.

function prototype   In C, a declaration of a function. Usually the term refers to an ANSI C declaration that specifies both the return value and the types and number of expected arguments, so that usage of actual arguments can be verified. Pre-ANSI C only allowed specification of the return value of a function, although the `lint` program was able to check argument types and number.

G

gateway

A computer that is endowed with hardware and software interfaces that enable it to route messages between networks.

To interconnect two or more networks, using a gateway.

glitch   A problem, often transient, in a hardware device. Also used occasionally to refer to software problems. Problems that are not well understood and not frequently encountered are often called *glitches*; when they are easily reproducible, they are called *bugs*.

global variables

Variables that exist for the lifetime of (during the entire period of execution) a program, in contrast to automatic variables, which are automatically created and destroyed as a program executes. Although usage varies, many people use the term to refer to data that is visible throughout a program.

In the Bourne shell, variables exist for the lifetime of the shell by default. However, each variable is confined to the shell unless it is explicitly exported, using the export command. The values of all exported variables are automatically made available to all programs that the shell executes.

In the C shell, variables exist for the lifetime of the C shell by default. However, variables are local to the C shell unless they are created with the setenv command. The values of all setenv-created variables are automatically made available to all programs that the C shell executes.

In C, variables declared outside of a function exist for the lifetime of a program, and they are visible throughout a program unless they are explicitly declared static. C static variables inside functions are only visible within their block, but they also exist for the lifetime of a program. *See also* storage class, extern; storage class, static.

globbing   An informal (but precise) term for performing the shell's filename generation process. This process is performed by the shell on modern systems, but in Version 6 UNIX this task was performed by the '/etc/glob' program. In the C shell the set noglob command turns off filename generation.

goto statement   A statement present in many programming languages that unconditionally transfers control to a specific location. In the Version 6 UNIX system the shell contained a goto statement as its only flow of control statement. The C shell contains a goto statement, but the Bourne shell does not. In assembly language, the goto statement is the basis of most programming. In C, a goto is present but not heavily used, because the more structured statements, if, while, for, and do, are preferred.

grammar   A set of rules that describes how the elements of a language may be combined. Programming languages usually have a very simple grammar, as compared to natural languages.

grap   An nroff/troff preprocessor that makes it easier to typeset charts and graphics. *See also* troff.

graphics   Relating to computer hardware and software that is used to create and manipulate diagrams and other visual displays.

graphic controller   A hardware interface that converts the information in a graphic display buffer into electrical signals that are appropriate for a given display screen. *See also* raster graphics; vector graphics.

graphic display buffer   A memory region that is connected to a CPU and to a graphic controller. The contents of the buffer are displayed, by the controller, on the display screen.

graphic terminal   A display terminal that is capable of displaying graphics. Some graphic terminals are connected to the computer via data links, and the graphic display process is controlled by a graphics description language. Other graphic terminals are directly connected to the memory system of the computer, so that the computer can write directly to the graphic display buffer.

grep

A UNIX program to search for text strings in text files. The grep program can search using for a group of strings, specified as ed-style regular expressions. Two related programs are egrep, which accepts an extended regular expression language, and fgrep, which can look for any string in a list of fixed strings. The term grep comes from the ed editor, whose command for searching through an entire file for lines that match a regular expression and then printing the matches is g/re/p where *re* is a regular expression.

To look for text patterns in files.

group   A set of UNIX users who are associated with a particular group number. A user's primary group membership is detailed in that person's entry in the '/etc/passwd' file, in the field following the user id number field. Groups are usually composed of users who are members of the same department, working on the same project, or related in other ways. Each UNIX file is associated with a particular group; members of that group have specified privileges for accessing files associated with that group. Group access privileges for files are displayed in the middle three characters of the nine character file access mode in a long format ls listing.

group id number   The number that specifies the group affiliation of a user. A group affiliation for each user is specified in the '/etc/passwd' file. The group affiliation of a file can be changed using the chgrp command. In System V, users can change their group id affiliation using the newgrp command. In Berkeley UNIX, users can simultaneously belong to more than one group, as specified in the '/etc/group' file. Often abbreviated *gid*.

guru An experienced, knowledgeable UNIX user.

H

hack

An expedient, but possibly short-term, solution. Used in a derogatory sense.

An informal term for creating software. In UNIX circles the term sometimes connotes a lack of seriousness or a lack of commitment. Authors of a program would not usually claim to be hacking while changing their own programs. However, people often claim to be hacking while making changes to other's software. Unlike its usage in other environments, *hacking* in UNIX circles does not imply illegal or malicious software activities, such as breaching system security.

A popular UNIX game.

hacker   An informal term for a programmer. UNIX hackers are noted for cleverness, flexibility, and doggedness, not for committing computer crime.

half-duplex   A characteristic of a communication system where information flows in one direction at a time. The direction of flow periodically reverses.

handler   *See* device driver.

hangup signal   A software signal that is sent to a process when the data line between the user and the computer is dropped, i.e. because the telephone has been hung up. Most processes exit when they receive the hangup signal, because in most cases a dropped data line means trouble, and the obvious remedy is to give up. To allow user's processes to continue to run after the user has logged off, the UNIX system has the nohup program, which makes its offspring processes ignore the hangup signal. Thus if you want to run a job in the background that continues after you log off, you should enter a command similar to the following.

```
$ nohup longjob > lj.out &
1802
$ _
```

In this example, the program called longjob is run in the background, immune to the hangup signal. If you run a job using nohup without explicitly redirecting its output, nohup arranges to route its output to a file called 'nohup.out'.

hard copy   User-readable, permanent computer output, usually on paper.

hard-copy terminal   *See* printing terminal.

hardware   The mechanical and electronic elements in a computer system.

hardwired terminal   Terminal attached to a computer by dedicated wires that provide a communication link between the computer and the terminal. The communication link between a computer and a hardwired terminal often has a greater bandwidth than that between a computer and a dial-up terminal.

hash   To compute a hashing function. *See* hashing.

hashing   Any of several techniques for deriving a numeric index from a text string. The result is that it becomes faster to scan an input for certain words. For example, hashing is often used in compilers so that they can more quickly recognize programming language keywords or subsequent instances of identifiers. Because most hashing functions are many to few maps, it is possible for two words to hash to the same result, which is called a *collision.* Several simple techniques can solve the problems caused by collisions. A hash that is guaranteed not to result in collisions is called a *perfect hash.* The UNIX C shell hashes the names found in directories mentioned in your search string, so that it can more rapidly locate commands. *See also* rehash.

81

header

A record at the beginning of a disk file. A header often details the size, location, and so on, of the information in the file. The UNIX kernel does not attend to the format of file headers; instead, individual applications subsystems create such standards. One exception is the header on executable files, which is used by the kernel when it loads the program for execution.

A special record or file at the beginning of a tape.

A preamble to a message in a communication system. Message headers often contain length information, sequence numbers, message format information, and routing information. The information content and layout of message headers is usually specified by standards organizations or committees.

header file   An alternate term for a C language include file. *See* include file.

here document   Temporarily redirected standard input within a shell program. The start of a here document is signaled with << symbol, followed by the text of the here document, followed by *symbol* on a line by itself. Programs are unaware that they are reading input from a here document; rather, they are reading as usual from the standard input. For example, the following fragment of a shell script shows how a here document is used to enable a message for the `mail` program to be placed in the script alongside the command to execute the `mail` program, rather than in a separate file.

```
    . . .
# now send completion message
mail opsmanager < <end
Please make a backup of the picture database filesystem
in the near future. The daily compression of that filesystem
has just completed normally.
end
# now clean up and exit
    . . .
```

See also I/O redirection.

hexadecimal character constant   A character constant specified as a hexadecimal value. In C, ordinary character constants are characters surrounded by single quotes, such as ´a´. Alternatively, characters can be specified by placing a hexadecimal number in quotes. This is especially useful for control characters and nongraphic characters. For example, ´\x61´ is a hexadecimal character constant that represents the same value as ´a´ (because the hexadecimal code for a lowercase *a* is 0x61). Also called a *hexadecimal escape sequence. See also* escape sequences, C.

hexadecimal constant   An integer numeric constant written in the hexadecimal number system. In C, such constants are always written with the prefix 0x (or 0X) followed immediately by the hexadecimal digits of the number.

hexadecimal escape sequence   *See* hexadecimal character constant.

hexadecimal radix   Base 16 numerical system. A hexadecimal number is written with the digits 0, 1, 2, 3, 4, 5, 6, 7, 8, 9, A, B, C, D, E, and F. In C language programs, hexadecimal numeric constants are written with a *0x* prefix; for example, 0x40 is the hexadecimal number 40.

hierarchy   System of persons or things that ranks or orders each item as above, below, or equal to each other item. The UNIX filesystem is hierarchical.

hierarchical filesystem   A scheme for storing files on a disk in which information is stored at different levels. In the UNIX filesystem, which is a hierarchical filesystem, each location in the filesystem is called a *directory*, and each directory is a collection of files and subdirectories. The start of each UNIX filesystem is a directory called the root directory.

high-level format   *See* format.

high-level language   Programming language that supports an abstract view of the process of computing, in contrast to assembly languages, which relate exclusively to a particular computer architecture. C, Fortran, BASIC, and Pascal are examples of high-level languages.

history   Record of the sequence of commands issued prior to the user's current command. On UNIX systems, the Korn and C shells have history mechanisms. The Korn shell uses an interactive system, which enables the user to browse through the list of previous commands interactively. The C shell history mechanism is a simple search-and-substitute language, which allows the user to specify and reuse bits of previous commands. C shell history substitutions are triggered by the ! character. On both shells the history information is kept in an ordinary file and thus is accessible to intruders. Don't supply crypt passwords on the command line if your shell is keeping a history file. *See also* argument list generation.

history mechanism   The capability of some shells and command systems to remember and reissue previously entered commands. *See also* history.

history substitution   An alteration of a command line to include text from a previous command. *See also* history.

hold buffer   An additional sed buffer for swapping text in and out of the sed pattern space.

hole (in a file)   A UNIX file can have a (conceptual) hole if it contains regions that have not been written to but have been bypassed by issuing the seek system call. The presence of the hole is recorded, but its content is not stored on disk and it does not occupy any space. A large file containing a hole may fit on a given filesystem, whereas a file of the same size but without the hole might not. During read operations, a hole in a file reads as if it had been filled with zeros.

hole (in a C structure)   *See* alignment.

$HOME   A Bourne shell variable that contains the name of your home directory.

$home   A C shell variable that contains the name of your home directory.

home directory   *See* directory, home.

HoneyDanBer UUCP   A version of the UUCP software written by Peter Honeyman, Dan Nowitz, and Brian E. Redman. *See* uucp.

host computer   Central computer being accessed by peripheral devices and possibly by other computers.

identifier In a programming language, a symbolic name for something. For example, a name for a constant, a variable, or a procedure.

IEEE The Institute for Electrical and Electronic Engineers. The IEEE is involved in various standardization efforts that affect UNIX, including the standardization of floating-point arithmetic.

IEEE floating point A standard for computations involving floating-point numbers.

#if In C, a preprocessor directive that controls conditional compilation. If the restricted constant expression following #if is true, then the following code is considered to be part of the program source. If it is false, then the following code is ignored. The region of code controlled by #if is delimited by #endif, and there may be #else and #elif (else if) statements in the region to further specify the conditional compilation. Restricted constant expressions may use the defined keyword to determine if certain identifiers are currently defined; this newer feature of C obviates the need for the original #ifdef (and #ifndef) directives. *See also* #ifdef; conditional compilation.

#ifdef, #ifndef In C, preprocessor directives that controls conditional compilation. If the following identifier is currently defined (for #ifdef, or undefined for #ifndef), then the following code is considered part of the program source; otherwise, the following code is ignored. The same capability can be achieved with the defined keyword and the #if preprocessor directive. *See also* #if; conditional compilation.

$IFS   A shell variable that holds the Bourne shell's current field separator characters. The usual field separators are a space, a tab, and a newline. You might want to change the field separators when you are dealing with records that use other field separators, such as the records in the '/etc/passwd' file. The name comes from the phrase *internal field separators*.

if statement   A component of many programming languages that allows you to selectively execute parts of a program based on the true/false status of an expression. In the Bourne and C shells you can selectively execute command lists based on the exit status of a conditional command. In C, you can selectively execute statements (or blocks) based on the value of an expression. *See also* conditional.

impact printer   A printer that uses a physical impact between print head and paper to create an impression on the paper. Impact printers usually use ribbons, in contrast to electrostatic printers, ink jet printers, laser printers, and phototypesetters, which avoid the mechanical action inherent in impact printers.

#include   In C, a preprocessor directive that includes the contents of a named file in the current compilation. If the filename is surrounded by double quotes, the compiler attempts to find it in the current directory. If the filename is surrounded by angle brackets, the C compiler attempts to find it in the standard include location, which is '/usr/include' on most UNIX systems. *See also* file inclusion; include file.

include file   A file containing information needed by several program modules. During compilation, the text of the include file becomes part of the program text that is analyzed by the compiler. Also called a header file. C language include files are customarily named using a *.h* extension, which is a reference to the term *header* file. *See also* #include.

incremental dump   *See* dump, incremental.

increment operator   *See* operator, increment.

indent

To move text in from the customary margin, as in the first line of some paragraphs.

The distance that text is moved in from the margins.

index   To create an ordered means of accessing a data set, somewhat like indexing a book to provide a way for people to look up specific information in a book.

index, array   An expression that selects a particular element in an array. Multidimensional arrays need one index expression for each dimension. Most indexes are integers, although some languages also support character indexes, enumeration indexes, and string indexes. In common use the plural is either *indexes* or *indices*, but *indexes* is preferred in technical usage.

indirect block   A block on a filesystem that contains the block numbers of the blocks of a particular file. For any given file, its i-node contains the disk block numbers of the first few (often ten) blocks of a file. If a file requires additional blocks, their block numbers are stored in an indirect block, whose block number is stored in the i-node. If additional indirect blocks are required, their addresses are stored in a double indirect block, whose block number is stored in the i-node. Similarly for triple indirect blocks. *See also* i-node; double indirect block; triple indirect block.

indirection   In C, to use pointer variables or address expressions to access data. The C language operator to access a value indirectly (via a pointer variable or address expression) is the *, which is often called the *dereference operator. See also* dereference operator.

init

The first real process created by the UNIX kernel at boot time. init always has the process id number one. The role of init is to maintain the multi-user state of the machine. init is the parent of all getty programs that are waiting for users to log in on a machine's communication lines. When someone logs in, getty exec's `login`, which (after password verification) exec's a login shell. Thus each login shell is a descendent of `init`. When a user logs off, `init` is notified of the death of a child and then spawns another `getty` to restart the sequence of events. `init` discovers a machine's I/O port configuration by reading the file '/etc/ttys'.

An informal abbreviation for initialize. *See* initialize.

initialization

The original assignment of a value to a variable. For external and static C language variables, initialization is usually performed on UNIX systems by placing the initial values in the program's memory region before the program starts to execute. For auto C language variables, the initialization usually is done by assignment commands that are automatically performed when the procedure is activated.

The process of setting up any system with a standard set of values or configuration, prior to normal operation of the system.

initialize   To perform or specify an initialization.

initializer   In C, a value (or group of values) that is used to specify an initial value for a variable in a definition. Initializers may be supplied for all `static` or external variables, but they may not be supplied for `extern` declarations or for auto aggregates (auto arrays, structures, or unions).

i-node   The essential internal structure for managing files in the UNIX filesystem. An i-node contains all the information pertaining to the mode, type, owner, size, and location (of the blocks) of a file; it does not contain the actual information that is stored in a file. A table of i-nodes is stored near the beginning of every UNIX filesystem. Because i-nodes have a fixed size, the system can locate an individual i-node given its i-node number. File names are related to particular i-nodes in directories, which contain an i-node number for each filename. Several filenames may point to the same i-node; they are all said to be *links* to the file, and each filename has equal precedence. An i-node number is unique within a given filesystem, and each filesystem is configured for a maximum number of i-nodes, which is a limit to the number of separate files in that filesystem.

i-node number   Number specifying a particular i-node on a filesystem. Each entry in a directory file consists of a filename and its i-node number. Sometimes written as i-number.

input

The information that a program acquires.

To acquire information.

input, standard   *See* standard input.

input redirection   Reassignment by the shell of a program's standard input to a file other than the terminal. The user activates input redirection by placing a < on the command line, followed by the name of the desired input file. For example, in the following dialogue a C shell is invoked to execute the commands in the given script.

```
$ csh < mkhisto.csh
$ _
```

See also standard input; standard I/O connections.

insert   To place information in the midst of existing information. For example, the vi text editor has a command that allows to you type new text in the midst of existing text.

insert mode   A mode of the vi editor that allows you to enter new information into a text file. Unlike append mode, in insert mode the information is added to the file in front of where the cursor was originally positioned. In vi you terminate insert mode by hitting the escape key.

install

With reference to hardware, to electrically and/or mechanically connect the hardware to a computer system.

With reference to software, to place the individual files into their assigned locations in the filesystem, to perform any site-dependent chores, such as recompiling site-dependent software modules, and to perform any other necessary chores to make the software operable on a given system.

instruction   One of the basic operations performed by a machine. Typical computers contain instructions to add two numbers, compare numbers, transfer information from one memory cell in the machine to another, and change the sequence of instruction execution.

instruction, computer aided   *See* computer-aided instruction.

int   A C language data type that corresponds to the natural word size on a given machine. C does not specify the size of (number of bytes required to store) an int, other than to guarantee that it is neither smaller than a short nor larger than a long.

integer   Positive or negative whole number. On 16-bit computers, integers are usually constrained to the range -32768 to 32767. On 32-bit computers, integers can usually attain values in the range -2147483648 to 2147483647.

interactive computer system   A conversational system allowing a continuous dialogue between the user and the computer. *See also* batch processing.

interface

An electrical device designed to facilitate communication between the computer and its peripherals. Also called a *controller*.

A software module that converts information or commands from one form to another.

The portion of an interactive software program that manages the user dialogue. Usually called the *user interface.*

To perform the necessary conversions so that two hardware or software systems can interact.

internet protocol   *See* IP.

interpret   To perform (in software) the instructions coded in a script or program. "This improved version of BASIC can interpret almost a thousand statements per second."

interpreter   A program that performs the instructions coded in a script or program. Most interpreters do not translate the instructions into the machine's native code; rather, they perform the instructions directly. Most interpreters can be controlled either interactively, or by a script. The most important interpreter on the UNIX system is the shell. The most widely known interpreter is probably the BASIC language.

interpreter, command   *See* command interpreter.

interpretive programming language   A programming language that can be executed through an interpreter, such as the shell programming language, and most versions of BASIC.

interrupt

In the computer hardware, an electrical signal that indicates a certain condition, such as the arrival of data at an interface, the expiration of a timer, or the completion of a data transfer. Most interrupts are generated by peripheral devices. When the electrical signal is activated, the computer suspends its current task and instead performs the instructions in an interrupt handler. The interrupt handler typically manages a time-critical, low-level aspect of the computer's operation. When the interrupt servicing is complete, the computer resumes the original task. Most computers have multiple interrupt sources, arranged in a priority system. The major role of interrupts is to enable the computer to supervise data transfers, although errors in peripheral devices often cause interrupts. Interrupt handlers for UNIX systems are part of each device driver. It is normally not possible for an ordinary UNIX process to manage a hardware interrupt; instead, they are handled by the UNIX.

To suspend an ongoing task, so that a more time critical task can be executed temporarily.

interrupt character   A keyboard character that you can strike to terminate the currently executing program. When you strike the interrupt character, the interrupt signal is sent to the process, which will terminate the process unless it has arranged to ignore or manage the signal. The interrupt character is often assigned to the Ctrl-C character, or to the DEL character, although it can be assigned to any keyboard character using the stty command. *See also* interrupt signal; erase character; kill character.

interrupt handler

In the UNIX kernel, a software routine that is executed as a result of a hardware interrupt, to service that interrupt. The exact chore performed by each interrupt handler varies; typical chores include acquiring data from the device, sending the next unit of data to the device, and responding to error conditions. Interrupt handlers are usually designed to do as little as possible, so that they operate as rapidly as possible, leaving the more difficult tasks for other parts of the software. In the UNIX system, an interrupt handler may be part of each device driver. Most UNIX interrupt handlers are named with the customary two-letter device name followed by the word *intr*. Thus the routine named hpintr is an interrupt handler for an *hp* disk interface. Also called an interrupt service routine.

In a UNIX program, a software routine that is called when a signal arrives. Also called a signal handler. *See also* signal handler.

interrupt signal   A software signal (number 2, called SIGINT) that can be sent to a process. Unless other provisions have been made by the receiving process, it will terminate when it receives the interrupt signal. At the user level, an interrupt signal can be sent to a specific process using the kill command. The interrupt signal can be sent to the current process by striking the interrupt character. *See also* signal.

int type   In C, an arithmetic data type that corresponds to the natural word size of the machine. On 32-bit computers, an int is a 32-bit value.

invisible character   A character that does not have a graphic representation. Often used to refer to a control character that has somehow become embedded in a filename or in a text file. Filenames sometimes acquire invisible characters because of typos, hardware failures, or software bugs. The -v option of cat unambiguously displays control codes in files. To detect invisible characters in a filename, pipe the output of ls to cat -v. Another method is to engage the -q option of ls (which is on by default in Berkeley systems, when output is to a terminal), which displays invisible characters in a filename as ?. There are several techniques for deleting or renaming a file whose name contains an invisible character; the most common is using wildcards.

ioctl A generic system call that is used to enable user programs to access specific UNIX kernel device driver features. For example, ioctls are used to manage terminal modes, such as tab expansion and special character assignments.

I/O (input/output)

Transmission of information between a computer and peripheral units such as mass storage devices, terminals, and printers. The UNIX kernel performs I/O to peripherals by invoking the services of its device drivers.

Transmission of information to/from an executing process. I/O requests by UNIX processes are converted, if necessary, by the kernel to I/O operations involving the peripherals.

I/O device Peripheral device to and/or from which information can be transmitted by the computer. Typical I/O devices are printers, terminals, disks, and network interfaces. In the UNIX system, processes access I/O devices by performing I/O operations on special files. The kernel responds to I/O requests on special files by accessing the actual I/O device hardware. It does this using its device drivers, each of which is written to manage a specific I/O device. *See also* special file.

I/O redirection Connecting a process' standard input, output, or error connection to somewhere other than the user's terminal. *See also* input redirection; output redirection; pipelines; here documents; standard I/O connections.

IP   A protocol for managing connections from one machine to another, often over more than one network or route. *IP* is an acronym for internet protocol. Often used in conjunction with TCP. *See also* TCP.

iterate   To repeatedly perform a single task, often in concert with a progressive change in the value of a variable. Also called *looping*.

iteration   One performance of a task that is performed repetitively.

iterative statements

In a programming language, control statements that cause other statements to be executed repeatedly. They are used to construct loops.

In the Bourne shell, the iterative statements are for, while, and until. *See also* for; while; until.

In the C shell, the iterative statements are foreach, repeat, and while.

In C, the iterative statements are do, for, and while. *See also* do; for; while.

J

job

Task for the computer to perform, generally a noninteractive task.

In Berkeley UNIX, a command or group of commands that can be suspended, killed, or moved to the background or foreground as a single unit.

job control　　A feature of Berkeley UNIX systems that allows a user to move processes back and forth between background and foreground. The principle commands are bg and fg, to switch jobs between background and foreground, and jobs, to list the current jobs. During the execution of most programs the user can strike the suspend character, which is usually Ctrl-Z, to suspend the current job and "wake up" the shell. Some interactive programs, such as vi, have built-in commands enabling the user to suspend them as necessary.

job number　　A small number used to identify a job in Berkeley's job control system. Job numbers are known only to the shell from which the jobs oriented, unlike a process id number, which is universally known.

Johnson, Stephen　　Author of the portable C compiler, and, with Dennis Ritchie, the first person to port the UNIX system (to the Interdata 8/32, in 1976).

Joy, William　　Author of the C Shell (csh), ex/vi, Berkeley Pascal, a major contributor to Berkeley UNIX, and a cofounder of Sun Microsystems.

justified text   Text that has interword (and possibly intercharacter) spacing adjusted so that each line is of a uniform length. This creates smooth left and right margins, which are required for some documents. The UNIX text formatters `nroff` and `troff` can produce justified text.

keep   In a `troff` document, a region that is kept together, so that it is not split into two by a page break. Keeps often hold together short tables, verses of poems, quotations, and the like.

kernel   The memory resident part of the UNIX operating system, containing all the UNIX system functions that are needed immediately and frequently. The kernel supervises I/O transactions, manages and controls hardware, and schedules user processes for execution. The Version 7 UNIX system kernel is compiled from about 10,000 lines of C language code and about 1000 lines of assembly language code. Newer kernels are larger. In the UNIX system, the kernel is endowed with relatively few features (compared to other operating systems), so that these features may be provided more conveniently and flexibly by individual utility programs.

Kernighan and Ritchie   A reference to Brian Kernighan and Dennis Ritchie, the authors of the original book on C, or to the book itself. Dennis Ritchie is the original designer of C. The book (*The C Programming Language*, Kernighan and Ritchie, Prentice Hall, Englewood Cliffs, NJ, 1978) is often referred to as *Kernighan and Ritchie* or simply as *K&R*. It is also sometimes called the *C Bible* or the *white book.* The version of C described in Appendix A of that book is often called *K&R C. See also* Kernighan, Brian W.; Ritchie, Dennis M.

Kernighan, Brian W.   Longtime contributor to UNIX software, including contributions to `troff` and `awk`, and coauthor of the original book on the C programming language.

key

One of the buttons on a keyboard.

A short text string that is used to encrypt or decrypt a document.

keystroke   The act of pressing a key on a terminal keyboard.

keywords   In a programming language, database system, or other computer language, words that have special meanings. Keywords usually implement the major constructs of a language, and they are usually reserved, meaning that they cannot be used as ordinary identifiers. For example, in C there are keywords for defining data and functions (int, float, static, extern, etc.), and keywords for controlling statement execution (if, while, return), plus a few miscellaneous keywords, such as sizeof, which returns the size of its operand.

kill

To send a software signal to a UNIX process. Processes can be killed using the kill command, which actually sends the signal using the kill system call. Signals often terminate a process, hence the name. *See also* signal.

A UNIX command that can send a signal to a process.

kill character   The special keyboard character that erases the entire current line, so that it may be retyped. Also called the line-erase character. On many systems it is initially assigned to the commercial at (@) key or to the Ctrl-U key; it can be reassigned to another key using the stty command. (*Note:* The kill character has nothing to do with sending the kill signal to a process.) *See also* interrupt character; erase character.

kill signal   A signal (number 9, also called *SIGKILL*) that can be sent to a process to ensure that it is terminated. Unlike many signals, the kill signal cannot be caught or ignored. Thus a process that receives the kill signal will, with a few minor exceptions, terminate immediately. Many processes, such as the standard text editors, need to perform exit processing to protect your data.

Because the kill signal cannot be caught or ignored, sending it to such a process is likely to result in data loss. Sending the kill signal to a process should be considered as a last resort, a technique that should be used only when all else fails. The usual signal to send to a process to cause its termination is the interrupt signal (number 2). Unlike the interrupt and quit signals, there is no keyboard character that can send the kill signal to a process. Rather, it can only be sent explicitly using the kill system call. The user-level command to send the kill signal is kill -9 *pid,* where *pid* is the process identification number of the target process. *See also* signal; interrupt signal.

Korn, David   Author of the Korn shell (ksh). Korn's shell is an enhancement of the Bourne shell, and it is a prime candidate for the next "standard" UNIX system shell. *See also* Korn shell.

Korn shell   David Korn's extension of the Bourne shell. The Korn shell is fully compatible with the Bourne shell, but it has several additional features that make it very attractive. Overall, it has much higher performance than the Bourne shell, it has a very convenient history editor that gives you a mini-vi or mini-emacs editor for editing and resubmitting past commands, it has C-shell-like job control, C-shell-like tilde substitution, C-shell-like aliases, shell functions (like newer versions of the Bourne shell), and new facilities for managing shell variables. On some systems the Korn shell is named *'/bin/sh',* which makes it the standard Bourne style shell. (On such systems the true Bourne shell is often named *'/bin/osh'.*) On other systems the Korn shell is available as *'/bin/ksh'.*

K&R   *See* Kernighan and Ritchie.

K&R C   A reference to the version of C specified in Kernighan and Ritchie's book *The C Programming Language. See also* ANSI C.

L

label, statement   A symbolic name to identify a location in a program. Control can be transferred to the labeled location by using a goto statement (called *jump* or *branch* in most assembly languages).

LAN   *See* local area network.

language   *See* programming language.

laser printer   A printer whose mechanism consists of a laser beam that projects an image onto a photosensitive drum, similar to the drum that is used in most office copiers. Then the drum is selectively inked, and the ink is mechanically fused onto paper. Laser printers can be relatively fast, and they can produce relatively high quality print. Typical resolution is 300 dots per inch. With appropriate software, such as the nroff/troff formatter, laser printers can sometimes substitute for typesetters, although their resolution is typically less than half that of typesetters. Laser printers vary widely in price; high-speed high-volume machines are expensive, while lower-speed, lower-volume machines are economical even for small installations.

lcase mode   A mode of the tty handler that allows one to work with the system using an uppercase-only terminal. If you mistakenly log onto the system with your terminal's caps lock key engaged, the system will notice your all-uppercase input and automatically engage lcase mode. One easy remedy is to log out and then log in again without the caps lock key engaged. Another remedy is to use the stty command to change the tty mode to –lcase, which is the normal mode of operation.

lex   A UNIX program that, based on a tabular specification, can create a C language or a Ratfor language lexical analyzer. The tabular specification describes the low-level objects that should be recognized, using a regular expression language similar to that of ed. Then the `lex` program translates the description into C or Ratfor source code that, when compiled, can recognize the given objects. `lex` makes it easy to develop a lexical analyzer, but other techniques can often produce a more efficient lexical analyzer. *See also* `yacc`.

lexical analysis   Examination and classification of the low-level objects in a program or command. The low level objects are often numbers, operators, variable names, and keywords. Lexical analysis is normally a sequential process that operates on a small, local group of characters in a stream of characters. UNIX contains a program generator named `lex` that simplifies the task of writing a lexical analysis program. *See also* parse; lex.

library   An ordinary file into which the contents of other ordinary files are placed. This collects a group of files into a single larger file, so that they can conveniently be accessed for some purpose. The most common libraries on UNIX systems are libraries of object files, which are accessed by the linkage editor during the final linkage of a program. Placing numerous object files into a single library speeds up and simplifies the operation of the compiler, because it can access all the information it needs in a single file. UNIX programming libraries are created and maintained by the `ar` program. Also called an archive.

line editor   *See* editor, line.

line-erase character   *See* kill character.

line feed   An ASCII character that advances most terminals or printers to the following line. The ASCII code for a line feed is octal 012 (decimal 10). On terminals that lack a line-feed key, a line-feed character can usually be generated by striking Ctrl-J.

line-oriented program   An interactive program or other interactive system whose dialogues tend to be based on lines of input and output. The Bourne and C shell are line-oriented command systems, the ed editor is a line-oriented text editor. A counterexample is vi, which is a screen-oriented text editor.

line printer   At one time this term was reserved for high-speed printers that output a line of text at a time, but in modern usage it simply refers to whatever printer is connected to the UNIX system spooler.

link

To combine object files to form a complete program. The UNIX linker is named ld, which is almost an acronym for linkage editor. Although ld can be invoked separately, it can also be invoked automatically as the final stage of most UNIX compilers. *See also* link editor.

A connection between a filename, as stored in a directory, and an i-node. Each name for a file is a link to the file. When a file is created, its first link (its original name) is created. Additional links can be created with the ln command, and individual links can be removed with the rm command (or rmdir for directories). A link count is maintained in the i-node. When the link count of an i-node drops to zero, the space allocated to that file is freed and the i-node is marked as free. Directory files always have at least two links, one for the name of the directory, which is stored in its parent directory, and one for the entry '.' (dot), which is stored in the directory itself. Directories that contain subdirectories contain one additional link per subdirectory because each subdirectory contains the entry '..' (dot dot) that refers back to the parent. The number of links to a file is displayed in the second field of a long format ls listing. You can discover whether two filenames refer to a single file using the -i option of ls, which displays i-node numbers for each file. If two filenames refer to the same i-node number, and if they are on the same filesystem, they refer to a single file. Ordinary links only work within a single filesystem and cannot be used to link directories. However, Berkeley symbolic links use a different mechanism, which can span multiple filesystems and link directories. *See also* symbolic link; unlink.

link editor   In UNIX, the ld program, which links the modules in a program to form a complete program. *See also* link.

lint

A UNIX program that performs usage checks on C programs beyond those performed by the C compiler. `lint` has a much more questioning attitude than the traditional UNIX C compiler. It is capable of finding unused variables, variables whose values are used before they are set, functions called with varying numbers of arguments, functions called with the wrong types of arguments, functions that both return and return a value, functions whose return value is sometimes used and sometimes ignored, and other difficulties. The original C compilers performed little or no usage checking beyond the minimum necessary to generate code. Subsequent C compilers, especially on systems other than the UNIX system, are often much more suspicious, and have taken over many of the functions performed by `lint`.

To use `lint` to analyze a program.

Lions, John   Author of *A Commentary on the Unix Operating System* (University of New South Wales, 1977), the first book to independently discuss UNIX. The book was a detailed discussion of the Version 6 source code, which was included.

Lisp   A high-level programming language, usually used for artificial intelligence applications. One of the most common Lisps available for UNIX systems is Berkeley's Franz Lisp. The name is derived from the phrase *list processing*.

list

A term used in discussions of the shell to refer to a sequence of pipelines. The simplest list is a single pipeline, which may itself be a single command.

To display the contents of a directory. The name *ls* is derived from the word *list*. *See also* `ls`.

load   To place a binary executable file into main memory to enable execution.

load average The amount of usage currently demanded from a computer system. Typically, a load average of 1 means the system has just as much work as it can perform, load averages less than 1 mean the system is sometimes idle, and load averages greater than 1 mean that each task gets a smaller timeslice than it needs.

loader A software mechanism for placing a program image into memory so that it can be executed. The UNIX system loader is a component of the kernel.

local-area network (LAN) A network of computers that are physically close, usually less than a mile apart, and connected by a high-speed hardware/software communication system. Ethernet is the most common UNIX LAN hardware.

local declaration A declaration that creates a local variable. In C, declarations that occur within a function are local declarations. *See also* local variable.

local variable

In most programming languages, a variable that can be accessed only from certain regions of a program. Usually, a local variable is only accessible within one subroutine. Local variables are often created when their subroutine is invoked, and they cease to exist when the subroutine terminates. *See also* local declaration.

In the Bourne shell, variables are local unless they are explicitly exported using the export command. Once exported, a variable is available to every command that the shell executes. The values of local variables are often passed as arguments to commands by typing a $ followed by the variable name.

In the C shell, variables created by set are local. Values of local variables can be passed as arguments to commands by typing a $ followed by the name.

In C, local variables are variables that are created within a subroutine. There are two types: auto and static. An auto local variable is created when the subroutine is invoked, and it ceases to exist when the subroutine returns. One copy of each auto variable exists for each currently active copy of the procedure. static local variables are created when the program starts to execute, and they exist for the lifetime of the program. Additional copies are not made if a subroutine is called recursively (more than one simultaneous activation). static local variables, like auto local variables, are visible (accessible) only within the procedure. static local variables have many uses, including keeping track of recursion depth, recording how often a procedure is invoked, and controlling special processing the first time a function is called.

logic

In hardware, circuitry that performs Boolean logic operations on electrical signals.

In software, sections of a program that contain Boolean expressions.

login

The procedure of entering your name and password, enabling the UNIX system to verify your right to use the system. After a successful login, the system presents a prompt and waits for your commands.

To enter your login name and password, so that you may gain access to the UNIX system.

login directory   *See* home directory.

login name   The name that a user uses during the login procedure. Your login name identifies you to the system. Some systems impose restrictions on login names, such as a minimum length, or forcing users to use their last name. Another common policy is to make the employee or student id number serve as a login name. The name of each user's home directory is often the same as that person's login name. For example, the home directory of a user known as *kc* might be '/usr1/kc'. Login names are catalogued in the '/etc/passwd' file. Also called *user name*.

login session   Usage of a computer, from the time of logging in on a specific terminal through logging off from that terminal.

login shell   The shell that is spawned when you first login, or (equivalently) any shell whose whose parent is the `init` process. When you exit from a login shell the `init` process is notified of the death of a child, and then `init` proceeds to spawn another `getty` process to manage the communication line. When a C shell detects that it is a login shell, it executes the commands in '~/.login' at the beginning of a session and the commands in '~/.logout' at the conclusion of the session. *See also* `gtty`; `init`.

logout

The process of terminating a login session.

To inform the system that you are ending a session and placing no further demands on the system through a particular terminal. The process is also called *logging out* or *logging off.*

long type   In C, an arithmetic data type that usually has at least 32 bits of precision. On most 16-bit computers, longs are 32 bits, which is twice the size of an int. On most 32-bit computers, both longs and ints are 32 bits.

loop

See iterate.

A construct in a programming language that can cause an instruction sequence to be repeatedly executed.

lowercase   A letter or word that is not capitalized.

low-level format   *See* format.

low-level I/O library   When C was first used on UNIX systems, its only I/O library was the standard set of UNIX system calls for managing I/O: `read`, `write`, `lseek`, `open` and `close`. Today these I/O functions are often called the *low-level I/O library*, to distinguish them from the portable (streams) I/O library. Although these

107

operations provide a powerful underpinning, they are not ideal for many purposes, and they are not universally portable. They are available on all UNIX systems and are supported by most versions of C on MS-DOS systems. *See also* portable C I/O library.

ls   A UNIX program that lists the contents of directories.

LSI (large-scale integration)   An electronic device, consisting of a semiconductor (usually silicon) on which thousands of electronic elements have been fabricated. Most computers make extensive use of LSI devices.

lvalue   An operand that can be assigned a value, and thus can appear on the left (hence the term) side of an assignment. In C, variables and pointers to variables are lvalues. Arrays, functions, and constants are not lvalues.

M

machine dependent A program, or a part of a program, whose operation relies on a particular machine architecture. All assembly language code is machine dependent. In high-level languages, programmers sometimes unwittingly assume a particular machine architecture. For example, C programmers often assume that the character data type is either signed or unsigned, depending on what machine they customarily use. Programs with such assumptions can be difficult to port to machines with the opposite orientation.

machine independent Usable on more than one type of computer; not specific to a single hardware design. One of the strengths of the C language, and hence of the UNIX system, is its relatively high degree of machine independence. Versions of C are available for virtually every current computer, and versions of the UNIX system are available for most computers. Programs written in C with the goal of machine independence are often highly machine independent. Some of the UNIX system itself is, of necessity, machine dependent, but the majority of the operating system code, including most of the kernel's code, can be adapted to various machines with little difficulty.

machine language The native language of a computer. Different computer systems have different machine languages. The ultimate output of any compiler or assembler is a file containing machine language instructions.

macro A short piece of text that, when processed by appropriate software, is expanded into a longer piece of text. Each macro must be defined, which means associating a long piece of text with a name. Subsequent to the definition, the macro can be expanded, which means that each appearance of the macro name is replaced by the full text of the macro. Macros are used for several reasons, including rendering programs or documents more readable or more uniform, increasing efficiency, and creating alternate syntactic or semantic software interfaces. Macros are commonly used in several situations, including programming and word processing. Many assemblers have a macro capability. This enables a programmer to define a macro to be a common instruction sequence, and then code that sequence simply by writing the name of the macro. The standard UNIX assemblers do not usually have a macro capability, because most assembly language on UNIX systems is written by the C compiler, not by people. The C language includes a macro facility, based on the #define preprocessor directive. A programmer can create a macro definition using #define, and then each time the macro name is encountered the defined text is inserted into the program. Another program that makes extensive use of macros is nroff/troff. Because the nroff/troff language is so detail oriented, people have developed several packages of macros that make it easier to produce standard document formats. The most common nroff/troff macro packages are -mm, -ms, -me, and -man. Macros are created in nroff/troff using the .de directive. The vi editor also contains a macro facility. Using the :map command, you can create a macro that is invoked by a single keystroke, or using the :ab command, you can specify a word that, when typed, will trigger a macro replacement. *See also* -ms; -mm; -me; -man; nroff; C preprocessor; macro assembler; macro arguments; macro definition.

macro assembler　An assembler that includes a macro capability. *See also* macro; assembler.

macro arguments　Information that appears in the text (source) along with the macro name, so that it can be inserted into the replacement text. Macro arguments make it possible to write more powerful macros because they allow the replacement text to contain fixed parts and varying parts. *See also* macro.

macro call　*See* macro invocation.

macro definition　A specification of the replacement text for a macro. *See also* macro.

macro invocation   A use of a macro's name in a source file. When this file is processed by appropriate software, the macro name is replaced by its replacement text. Also called a *macro call.*

macro package   Prepackaged set of commands to facilitate tasks on a computer. In the UNIX system, the term *macro package* usually refers to a set of high-level nroff/troff text-formatting commands. The built-in nroff/troff commands are very low level and inconvenient; macro packages introduce a more convenient set of text processing functions. The four most common nroff/troff macro packages are -ms, the original word processing macro package; -mm, AT&T's comprehensive word processing package; -me, Berkeley's macro package; and -man, a macro package for manual page entries. *See* troff.

magic   Something that is incanted, sprinkled, or otherwise applied to make something work. Often used by gurus.

magic character   A character with a special meaning. The term is usually used to describe characters that have powerful, but sometimes difficult to understand, meanings. For example, the shell uses the *, ?, and [] characters to control the filename generation process. These magic characters must be quoted if you want to use them as ordinary characters, not as metacharacters. The C shell has an option setting that allows you to disable most magic shell characters, and the vi editor has the nomagic mode to allow you to disable its regular expression magic characters. Also called a *metacharacter.*

magic number   A number that is agreed on to represent some condition, and whose value is unusual for a given context. The most important example in the UNIX system is the magic number that appears at the head of binary executables and at the head of some shell scripts on Berkeley systems. At the front of a binary executable file, the magic number informs the kernel that the file contains an executable program image, and the specific value of the number tells the kernel whether text is shared, and so on. Magic numbers to indicate binary executable images are chosen carefully so that they could never occur as the first few bytes in a text file. Of course, the magic numbers could appear as the first values in a binary data file, but that event would be rare. On

Berkeley systems the magic number that identifies command scripts is followed by the name of the script, so that the kernel can exec the proper interpreter for the script. *See also* token, shell program.

magnetic tape   Linearly accessible storage medium for computer-readable information. The tape is usually made of mylar (plastic) and coated with magnetic oxide. On UNIX systems magnetic tape is primarily used to perform backups, and to import and export data. The dd program is often used for copying raw data, entire filesystems, and the like to magnetic tape. Two more sophisticated programs, tar and cpio are also commonly used to create or read magnetic tapes. When writing to a magnetic tape, both tar and cpio combine individual files into one larger file, which is then written to the tape. When reading a tape, tar and cpio can retrieve individual files or the entire contents of the tape. The principal advantage of tar is that its tape directory information is in ASCII, which makes tar tapes highly portable. One advantage of cpio is that it has features that make it easy to perform periodic backups to tape. Magnetic tape is also called *mag tape. See also* tar; cpio.

mail

See electronic mail.

To send electronic mail.

main   In C, the first user-written routine that is invoked when a program starts to execute is called main. Except that it is called first, it is no different than other functions in a program. Standard arguments are supplied to main so that C programs can access command line arguments. *See also* main, arguments; *argc*; *argv*.

main, arguments   On all UNIX systems, and on many other systems (such as most MS-DOS implementations), standard variables are passed to the C main routine so that it can access command-line information and the environment. The first two parameters are a count of command-line arguments, and a pointer to a list of pointers to the argument text. Each word in the argument list, starting with the name of the command, resides in a separate null-terminated string. Although any names may be chosen, many programmers name these two parameters argc (argument count) and argv (argument vector). The third argument, which is less often used and not always available, is a pointer to the program's environment. A more convenient interface to the program's environment strings is the commonly available getenv subroutine. *See also* main; *argc*; *argv*.

mainframe   A large, multi-user computer.

main memory   A unit capable of storing moderate quantities of information in a form that is accessible very rapidly by the CPU. Most modern computers use dynamic memory technology for their main memory because it is the most dense and cost effective. The size and access time of main memory is a major factor in the performance of a computer. UNIX systems work best with large amounts of main memory because greater amounts of memory enable the kernel to contain more buffers and reduce swapping. Main memory is occasionally called the *primary store*.

maintenance contract   An agreement between a computer owner and a computer service organization that stipulates terms and conditions for maintaining and repairing computer systems. A time-and-materials agreement specifies an hourly rate that is applied when repair or maintenance is necessary. A standard flat-rate service agreement specifies a single fee, which covers repairs during standard business hours. A 24-hour flat-rate service agreement also specifies a single fee, but the maintenance provider must respond promptly any time of the day or night.

major device number   The device-type classification of a block special or character special file. The major device entry selects a particular entry in the cdevsw or bdevsw kernel table, thus the major device number is the mapping from a name in the filesystem (a special file) to a particular device driver, and from there to a particular I/O device. The major (and minor) device numbers of special files are displayed in place of the size field in a long format ls listing. You can determine the major device numbers for the I/O devices on your machine by looking at the configuration files or in your system documentation. You need to know the major device number to run the /etc/mknod program to create (or re-create) special files. *See also* minor device number; special file.

make

A programmer's utility program to automate the compilation process. make is given a specification (in a file called a *makefile)* of the relationships in a software system and a set of rules for recreating out-of-date files. Each time you run make it analyzes the contents of a makefile, and then determines the modification times of the listed files. Finally, make issues the necessary commands to bring obsolete files (often object modules) up to date (often by running the compiler). make is especially helpful in large software systems. *See also* makefile.

To perform the compilation, assembly, linking, and other steps necessary to create an executable program from source code modules, often using the make utility.

makefile   A make specification file that contains information on program module dependencies. *See also* make.

malloc

A C subroutine that manages a memory heap. Executing programs access this storage by calling malloc, which allocates a part of the heap and then returns a pointer to the allocated memory. Storage can be returned to the heap by calling free.

To dynamically allocate memory, usually by calling malloc or one of its siblings.

-man   An nroff/troff macro package for formatting UNIX manual page entries. *See also* macro; troff.

man   A program that prints citations from the on-line manual. Not available in modern versions of System V or most smaller UNIX systems.

man page   *See* manual page.

manual page   The citation in the UNIX manual (or in the on-line manual) that describes a program or other feature of the system. The first place to look to find out about something.

manual page macros   *See* -man.

manuscript macros   *See* -ms.

marked-up document   A file containing text interspersed with formatting codes (the *marks*), such as nroff/troff codes. *See also* troff.

mass storage device   A hardware unit, usually a disk, tape, or cartridge, for storing large amounts of computer-readable information. The information residing on mass storage devices is accessible to the CPU, although access time is much longer than that for information stored in main memory. Information is stored magnetically on most mass storage devices, although optical and other technologies have been developed. Occasionally called the secondary store.

math library   A subroutine library containing subroutines to compute standard mathematical functions, such as *sin, cos,* and *ln.*

-me   An nroff/troff macro package for formatting documents. Developed by Eric Allman while he was at Berkeley, -me is probably the best designed and best documented macro package. -me supports all common preprocessors, including refer. Available on Berkeley UNIX systems. *See also* macro; troff.

media   Tapes, disks, diskettes, and other devices that are inserted into computer peripherals such as disk drives and tape drives to store information. On many storage devices, the media are removable. The singular is medium.

member selection   In C, structures and unions contain members. To access an individual element of a structure or union, you must use the member selection operator, which is a period. For example, if s is a structure, one of whose members is named x, then the expression s.x accesses the x member. If p is a pointer to a structure (the same type as s), then the expression (*p).x accesses the x member of the structure pointed at by p (the parentheses are necessary because of the C precedence rules). As a shortcut for this second expression, C offers a member selection operator for pointers, the -> operator. The expression p->x is equivalent to that shown above; it accesses the x member of the structure pointed at by p.

memorandum macros   *See* -mm.

memory   An electronic device that is able to hold information for high-speed storage, copying, and retrieval. Often the term refers to a computer's main memory. In the past, memory was often fabricated from magnetic cores, which could be magnetized in one of two orientations. Today there are several common memory technologies, all of which are based on semiconductors. *See also* core memory; dynamic memory; static memory; read-only memory; programmable read-only memory.

memory fault   A software error that is detected by many versions of the UNIX system. Memory faults occur when a program attempts to access memory that is outside its allocated data region. When a memory fault occurs, the kernel sends a signal to the process, and then the process terminates with a core dump, unless it has arranged to catch that signal. *See also* signal.

memory management   Techniques for allocating, freeing, and mapping computer memory to meet the requirements of executing processes. The kernel manages memory in UNIX systems.

memory management hardware   Computer hardware that is specifically designed to allow flexible allocation of memory to processes and to enhance the security of the system by preventing processes from accessing memory outside their allocated regions. Simple memory management hardware maps addresses generated by processes to specific physical locations in a computer. More sophisticated memory management hardware can also detect references to not-currently-resident memory, initiate software to page in the referenced pages, and then reperform the desired access.

memory resident   Currently in main memory. The kernel (instructions and data structures) is the only part of the UNIX system that is always memory resident. Executing processes are either memory resident, or temporarily stored in swap space.

menu   A screen display that lists available choices. There is usually an easy method for picking one of the selections, such as typing its number or moving the cursor to its location.

MERT   designed for real-time applications.

metacharacter   A symbol that has a special meaning in certain situations. For example, while entering shell commands the asterisk can be used to match any sequence of characters in a filename. Thus a word such as *.c tells the shell to generate a list of all files whose names end in a period, followed by c. Users wishing to enter metacharacters without invoking their special meanings must escape them or use quotation. Also called *wild card.*

microcomputer   Small, usually single-user, computer. Usually based on a single-chip microprocessor. Microcomputers that are used by an individual are often called *personal computers.*

microprocessor   A CPU that is fabricated with LSI (or better) technology so that the entire unit is on one (or a few) chips, rather than a CPU that is fabricated by interconnecting many standard logic elements on a circuit board. *See* chip; CPU.

minicomputer   Midsize computer, intermediate between mainframe and microcomputer in terms of complexity, cost, and performance. Minicomputers may be single-user or multi-user. The UNIX system was originally designed to operate on minicomputers.

minor device number   Part of the device number stored in the i-node of a block special or character special file. When I/O requests are made via special files, the minor device number is passed to the device driver. Most device drivers interpret the minor device driver as a request to perform I/O on a particular channel or connection, but others may use minor device numbers to select a particular operating mode. For example, the minor device number on a terminal's special file usually indicates which communication line. Minor device numbers (and the major device number) are displayed when you make a long format listing of a special file using the ls program. *See* special file; major device number.

-mm   The manuscript macros. This is the most elaborate general-purpose nroff/troff macro package. It features robust error diagnostics, flexible customization, and rich support for lists. It supports the tbl and eqn preprocessors, but not the refer preprocessor. It is the standard text-formatting macro package on System V, but it is often available on Berkeley systems. *See also* macro; troff.

mode   A state of a system. Many programs have modes, and different modes often have access to different commands. For example, in the vi text editor you can be in visual command mode, in visual text entry mode, or one of several other modes. In such software packages, it is important to always know what mode is active and to know how to switch from one mode to another. Some people prefer software that has few modes because they find it less confusing. *See also* modeless, text entry mode, command mode.

model   *See* regular expression.

modeless   A system that has few (or perhaps no) operating modes. The emacs text editor is often said to be modeless. *See also* mode.

modem   A device that translates data signals from a form compatible with data processing equipment into a form that can be transmitted long distances, usually over public telephone lines. Devices called *modems* are also used to extend the distance over which direct connect terminals can be connected to a computer. The term *modem* is derived from the word *modulator – demodulator*, which is an electrical engineering term for the signal transformation performed by a modem. *See also* acoustic coupler; direct connect modem; dial-up terminal.

mount

In UNIX, to make a filesystem accessible, by running the /etc/mount program.

To place a tape on a tape drive, or occasionally to place a disk in a disk drive.

mounted A filesystem that is logically connected to the active filesystem on a running UNIX system. When a UNIX system is first booted, only the root filesystem is accessible. During the transition to multi-user operations, the '/etc/rc' script often specifies that additional filesystems must be mounted so that their files and directories can be accessed. Mounting is accomplished with the /etc/mount program, which mounts a filesystem onto a given directory. After the mount, the filesystem's root directory is accessible in place of the given directory.

mount point The directory where a filesystem is mounted. For example, if the *'/dev/hp0b'* filesystem contains the */usr* filesystem, it is mounted on the '/usr' directory, which is its mount point. Mount points are listed by the /etc/mount command.

mount table The table that describes mounted filesystems, '/etc/mtab'. The contents of '/etc/mtab' are displayed by the /etc/mount command.

-ms The manuscript macros. -ms was the first general purpose nroff/troff macro package. It supports many documentation styles, and all common preprocessors, including refer. Although the newer macro packages (-me, -mm) have advantages over -ms, it is still widely used. Most of the original UNIX documentation was written with -ms. Always available on Berkeley systems, and often available (although unsupported) on System V. *See also* macro; troff.

MS-DOS A computer operating system for personal computers. MS-DOS was originally developed by Seattle Computer systems, and it was heavily influenced by the CPM-80 operating system. Later versions of MS-DOS have been developed by Microsoft Corporation, in cooperation with IBM, and later versions (2.0 on) have been heavily influenced by ideas from the UNIX system.

119

MTTR   Mean time to repair. A characteristic of a computer system that specifies the average time it takes to repair a malfunction. MTTR figures are usually determined by the manufacturer of a system.

Multics   An early experiment in interactive computing. Many ideas from Multics found their way into UNIX. Bell Laboratory's withdrawal from the Multics project was part of the zeitgeist that triggered Ken Thompson's early experiments with what has become the UNIX system.

multidimensional array   *See* array, multidimensional.

multiplexer   A device that transmits several electrical signals concurrently by interleaving and later reassembling the individual signals.

multiprocessor   A computer system that contains multiple main processors. Versions of the UNIX system are available for multiprocessors.

multiprogramming   *See* multitasking.

multitasking   Running several programs or routines simultaneously on a single computer. On UNIX systems, multitasking is accomplished by dividing each second into many smaller slices of time and then allocating execution time slices to each active process, based on priorities.

multi-user   Pertaining to a system that is able to support several users simultaneously. To accomplish this, the computer must obviously support multitasking, but the converse (multi-user capabilities on a multitasking computer) is not required. Because of the additional work that an operating system must do to manage multiple users (scheduling time and resources, providing security, managing multiple I/O transactions), a multi-user operating system is usually many times more complex than a single-user operating system. The original version of the UNIX system was multi-user, but still smaller than many single-user operating systems of the time.

N

naked machine   The hardware only of a computer, with no operating system or other programs to help the user. The naked machine can be controlled only through machine or assembly language.

named pipe   *See* FIFO.

negate   To compute the opposite or the negative of an expression.

network   A group of computers able to communicate at high speed and/or over long distances via special hardware and software connections. *See* wide-area network; local-area network.

network disk   A disk or a region of a disk that is physically connected to one system but made available to other systems via a computer network. In Sun networking terminology, a network disk is a region of one computer's disk that is dedicated to a diskless workstation, as its private disk region.

network filesystem   A filesystem that is present on the disk of one computer but made accessible to other systems via a network. *See also* RFS; NFS.

network server   A computer the provides resources, such as access to files, access to communications, or access to printers, on a computer network. Also called a *server*.

neqn   An `nroff` preprocessor that makes it easier to format mathematics on ordinary printers. *See also* eqn; `troff`.

NFS (network filesystem)   A software protocol, developed by Sun Microsystems, that allows computers to transparently share files over a local area network. *See also* diskless node; file server.

nice

A UNIX utility program that allows user's to reduce the priority of their processes. (The superuser can use nice to run processes at increased priority.)

The amount by which a process' priority has been altered by nice. For example, "Even though that troff job has a nice of ten, it is still slowing down the whole system."

To alter (usually to reduce) the priority of a process, by using the nice utility.

nroff   A text formatter that is available on all UNIX systems. nroff accepts the same document format specifications and uses the same macro packages as troff. The difference is that nroff is designed to send output to ordinary printers, while troff is designed to send output to typesetters or to laser printers. *Pronounced* en-roff. *See also* troff; macro.

null   Empty or nonexistent.

null argument   A command line argument that has no value, or an argument whose value is the null string. Such arguments are occasionally needed as placeholders, so that a program correctly interprets subsequent command-line arguments.

null device   The UNIX system null device is called *'/dev/null'*. When output is directed to the null device, it is discarded; when input is read from the null device end of file, it is immediately encountered. Output occasionally is directed to the null device to discard it; input occasionally is read from the null device to read nothing. Sometimes called a *bit bucket.*

null pointer   In C, a pointer whose bit pattern is all zeros. C guarantees that pointers to valid data never have an all zeroes bit pattern. Null pointers are the standard error return for procedures that return pointers. For example, the malloc procedure returns a null pointer if it is unable to satisfy a memory allocation request. Failure to check for null pointer return values is a common C programming error.

null string   Text string that does not contain any text. The length of a null string is zero.

null terminated   A list whose last member is identifiable because it is null (zero). In C, strings are customarily null terminated.

number register   A nroff/troff storage location, that can be used to store a numeric value. For example, all the standard macro packages keep the current section number in a number register. Each time the user starts a new section, the macro package increments the number register, and uses its value in the section heading.

object file   A file that contains machine language instructions that can be executed by a computer. In the UNIX system, an object file is usually the result of a compilation. Object files often don't contain a complete program, but only a program fragment. Multiple object files must be combined (linked) to form a complete program.

octal character constant   A character constant specified as an octal value. In C, ordinary character constants are characters surrounded by single quotes, such as ´a´. Control characters and nongraphic characters can be specified by placing an octal number in quotes. For example, ´\141´ is an octal character constant that represents the same value as ´a´ (because the octal code for a lowercase *a* is 141). Also called an *octal escape sequence. See also* escape sequence, C.

octal constant   An integer numeric constant written in the octal number system. In C, such constants are always written with the prefix 0 followed immediately by the octal digits of the number.

octal escape sequence   *See* octal character constant.

octal radix   Base eight numerical system. The digits of an octal number are 0, 1, 2, 3, 4, 5, 6, and 7. In C programs octal constants are written with a leading zero; thus 012 is an octal number, which is equal to decimal ten.

open

An I/O system call that is used to activate an I/O connection. The complementary system call is close.

Pertaining to an I/O connection that has been opened and not yet closed. For example, "the shell provides three open files for each process."

To activate an I/O connection, by using the open system call. For example, "the system crashes when my program opens '/dev/mem' for writing."

open-line editing   Editing a single line of a file without concurrent display of preceding and following lines. A capability of the ex/vi editor. A simplified form of visual editing.

operand   An item whose value and type is used in an expression in a manner specified by the expression's operators. In C, operands may be constants, variables, function calls, or combinations of these items. For example, in the expression x + 5 * y, the basic operands are x, 5, and y, but the expression 5 * y is also an operand (of the + operator).

operating system   A program for managing the resources of a computer. Operating systems simplify housekeeping duties such as I/O procedures, process scheduling, and filesystem management. User programs can access the computer's resources only under the direction of the operating system.

operator

A symbol, usually in a computer program, that specifies an arithmetic, logical, or other manipulation of its operands. Unary operators have one operand, binary operators have two operands, and tertiary operators have three operands. The C language is famous for its large assortment of operators.

A person who is employed to perform many of the routine tasks in the operation of a mid- to large-size computer facility. Operators commonly perform backups, assist hardware maintenance personnel, install new software, and help with simple user problems.

operator, address of   In C, a unary prefix operator that takes the address of its operand. If x is an integer variable, then the value of the expression &x is the address of x and its type is *pointer to integer.*

operator, arithmetic An operator that performs arithmetic manipulations on its operands, such as addition, subtraction, multiplication, and division.

operator, assignment In C, an operator that changes the value of one of its operands. C has two unary assignment operators, ++ and -- (increment and decrement), and 11 binary assignment operators. A binary assignment operator takes the value of its right operand and places it into the location indicated by its left operand. The left operand must be an lvalue. C is unusual because assignment is performed by an operator and is thus a component of an expression, unlike most languages that consider assignment to be a fundamental type of statement. C has a simple assignment operator (=), plus ten compound assignment operators. A compound operator involves its left operand in the expression. For example, the expression x += y means that x should be added to y, and then that value should be stored in x. This would be written as x = x + y in many other languages. C contains the following compound assignment operators: -=, +=, *=, /-, %=, >>=, <<=, &=, | =, and ^=. *See also* operator, increment; and operator, decrement.

operator associativity A characteristic of an operator that determines the order in which expressions having adjacent operators of equal precedence are evaluated. Operators associate either left to right, or right to left. For example, in C the addition and subtraction operators have equal precedence, and they associate left to right. Thus in C the expression 5 - 4 + 3 has the value 4 because it is equivalent to (5 - 4) + 3. In a language that had right to left associative (and equal precedence) addition and subtraction, the expression 5 - 4 + 3 would be equivalent to 5 - (4 + 3) and thus have the value -2. C operators associate left to right except for the following: unary minus, bitwise and logical complement, indirection, address of, increment and decrement, sizeof, casts, conditional (tertiary), and assignment.

operator, binary An operator with two operands. In C, binary operators are placed between the two operands.

operator, bitwise   An operator that manipulates the individual bits of its operands.

operator, comma   A C language operator that causes its two operands to be evaluated; first the left operand and then the right operand. The result is the value and type of the right operand. Unlike most C operators, the order of evaluation of the comma operator is guaranteed to be left to right. The comma operator is used principally to place two (or more) expressions in a place where only a single expression is allowed. For example, in a for loop there are three control expressions. By using a comma operator, it is possible to insert more than expression into each place.

```
for(i=0, j=0, k=0; i < 10; i++, j--, k*=2)
    . . .
```

In this for loop, the initialization part sets i, j, and k to zero, the test part checks to see if i is less than ten, and the increment part performs three separate operations on the variables. Beware that in declarations a comma is used to separate items in lists, and in procedure calls it is used to separate the items in the argument list. The comma operator is also called the sequential evaluation operator.

operator, decrement   In C and awk, an operator to decrement its operand. The C language decrement operator is --, which may be placed before or after its operand. It operates similarly to the increment operator. *See also* operator, increment; operator, assignment.

operator, increment   In C and awk, an operator to increment its operand. The C language increment operator is ++, which may be placed before or after its operand. When placed before, the increment is performed before the value of the operand is used in the expression; when placed after, the original value of the operand is used in the expression, and then the increment occurs. When the increment operator is applied to pointers, the pointer is made to point at the next object in memory. For example, incrementing a pointer to a double makes it point at the next double. Thus, incrementing pointers does not, generally, add one to the address stored in the pointer. Rather, the address is increased enough to access the next item pointed at. This works analogously to array

127

indices; adding one to an array index accesses the next item (of whatever size) in the array. *See also* operator, assignment.

operator, indirection In C, a unary prefix operator (*) that accesses the address pointed to by its operand. For example, if p is a pointer to integer, then the expression *p accesses whatever integer p is pointing at.

operator, logical An operator that performs logical manipulations on its operands, such as comparing operands, and performing Boolean operations such as AND, OR, and NOT. C guarantees that logical operations proceed from left to right, and it further guarantees that logical operations only proceed as far as is necessary to determine the value of the expression. Thus in the expression a && b, the variable b will not be evaluated if a is false; in the expression a || b, the variable b will not be evaluated if a is true. *See also* short circuit evaluation.

operator overloading To assign an additional meaning to an operator. For example, the + symbol normally signifies addition. In a language that supports operator overloading the + might also be defined to symbolize the set union operation when it is applied to two arrays. When operators are overloaded, their meaning is usually inferred from the types of their operands. In the example just mentioned, the expression x + y specifies simple addition if x and y are simple variables, but it specifies the union operation if x and y are arrays.

operator precedence A characteristic of an operator that determines the order in which expressions involving operators of differing precedence are evaluated. Operations involving operators of higher precedence are performed first. For example, in C, the multiplication operator has precedence over the addition operator. Thus the expression x + 5 * y is equivalent to x + (5 * y).

operators, C The C language is known for its rich assortment of operators. The following table summarizes the operators.

Arithmetic

+	Addition (binary)		–	Subtraction (binary)
+	Force order of evaluation (unary)		–	Negation (unary)
++	Increment		– –	Decrement
*	Multiplication		/	Division
			%	Remainder

Logical

==	Equality		!=	Not equal
<	Less than		>	Greater than
<=	Less than or equal		>=	Greater than or equal
&&	Logical AND		||	Logical OR
!	Logical NOT			

Bitwise

&	Bitwise AND		|	Bitwise OR
~	Bitwise complement		^	Bitwise exclusive OR
<<	Left Shift		>>	Right Shift

Assignment

=	Assign		^=	Assign bitwise exclusive OR
&=	Assign bitwise AND		|=	Assign bitwise OR
<<=	Assign left shift		>>=	Assign right shift
+=	Assign sum		–=	Assign difference
*=	Assign product		/=	Assign quotient
			%=	Assign remainder

Miscellaneous

*	Indirection		&	Address of
,	Sequential evaluation		? :	Conditional (tertiary)
sizeof	Size of type or variable		(type)	Type cast
.	Member of		–>	Member pointed towards
[ ]	Element of array		( )	Parentheses

operator, tertiary   An operator with three operands. In C, there is only one tertiary operator, which is also called the *conditional operator*. Its result is one of two expressions, depending on the value of a test expression. The tertiary operators test expression is followed by a ?, followed by two expressions separated by a :. When the test expression is true, the result is the first expression; otherwise, the result is the second. For example, the value of the expression x ? 10 : 20 is ten if x is true, and twenty if x is false.

operator, unary   An operator that manipulates a single operand. C contains the following unary operators: unary minus, unary plus, bitwise and logical complement, indirection, address of, increment and decrement, sizeof and casts. The increment and decrement operators can be either prefix or postfix operators; the others are all prefix operators.

optimize   To improve something, often a software program. Software is often written initially as simply as possible. Later, when the needs and characteristics of the system are better known, key routines are optimized to improve their performance or to decrease their storage consumption, and so forth.

optimizer   A feature of many compilers that attempts to produce better code. Compilers can optimize to minimize the consumption of either (storage) space or (execution) time. Many compilers leave optimization off by default because it slows execution of the compiler.

option   An argument that alters the operation of a command; also called a flag in UNIX or a switch or control in other operating systems. In the UNIX system, options are usually single characters preceded by a hyphen. For example, in the UNIX command ps -1, the option is the letter *l*, which directs the ps command to produce a long format list of processes rather than the usual short format list.

order of evaluation   The sequence in which a computer performs the operations indicated by an expression. The precedence and associativity of the operators in an expression controls the grouping, but in C, the order of evaluation is usually determined by the C compiler. The order of evaluation is most important when expressions have side effects, or when the programmer is attempting to control precision or prevent overflow or underflow during arithmetic operations. In C, the following operators do guarantee their order of evaluation. The comma operator guarantees that its left operand is evaluated before its right operand, and the logical AND and OR operators guarantee left to right evaluation of their operands. In ANSI C, there is a unary plus operator, which can be used to force a component of an expression to be evaluated as a unit. For example, in the expression a + +(b + c) the unary plus (the second +) guarantees that b is added to c, and then that result is added to a. Without the unary plus the C compiler is free to perform the addition of a, b, and c in any order.

ordinary file   Ordinary files are used for storing data and instructions. Ordinary files often contain programs, documents, letters, databases, and other types of information. Ordinary files are identified by a hyphen in the first column of a long format ls listing. *See also* file.

orphan

See orphaned file.

A line of text stranded at the top of a page. It is called an "orphan" because the remainder of its paragraph is at the bottom of the preceding page. The nroff/troff formatter can avoid widows, but it is not very good at managing orphans. *See also* widow.

orphaned file   A file whose name has been lost, but whose content remains. Orphaned files occur when the UNIX filesystem is damaged. They are typically placed into the 'lost+found' directory by the fsck filesystem repair utility.

orphaned process   A process whose parent has exited. An orphaned process can never become a zombie process, because when an orphaned process exits, its slot in the process table is immediately released. (When processes that are not orphans exit, they tie up a slot in the process table until their parent waits for them or exits.) *See also* zombie.

other   A UNIX user is categorized as *other* for the purpose of determining access rights to a file when that person does not own the file and does not belong to the file's group.

output

Data resulting from a command or process. The term often refers to text that is sent to a program's standard output, although the result of a compilation, which does not appear on the standard output, could also be called *output*.

To produce output.

output redirection   Reassignment by the shell of a program's standard output to a file other than the terminal. On a command line, output redirection is invoked by writing the > character, followed by the name of the desired output file. For example, the following shell command directs the output of the who command into a file named 'wlist', and then looks at that output using the cat program.

```
$ who > wlist
$ cat wlist
gilbert    ttyh1  May 3 15:02
torsten    ttyh0  May 1  8:02
colin      ttyia  May 2  9:40
$ _
```

See also standard I/O connections; input redirection.

output, standard   *See* standard output.

output, standard error   *See* standard error output.

overflow

A condition that arises when the result of an expression is too large to be represented in the indicated data type. Overflow of floating-point expressions can cause a signal to be sent to a process or termination of a process. Overflow of integral expressions isn't detected by most computer systems.

For data to arrive faster than it can be managed by the receiver, leading to data loss.

overloading   Having more than one meaning for a given symbol. Many programming languages have overloaded operators. The specific operation performed depends on the types of the operands. In C, the (), ,, &, *, +, -, and . symbols are overloaded. Parentheses manage the order of evaluation in expressions, surround type names in type casts, and surround arguments in function argument lists. The , usually indicates sequential evaluation, except in argument lists or in declarations, where it is a separator. The & indicates bitwise AND when used as a binary operator, but it takes the address of its operand when used as a unary operator. The * indicates multiplication when used as a binary operator, but indirection when used as a unary operator. The + and - operators indicate addition and subtraction when used as binary operators, but + forces evaluation order and - performs negation when used as unary operators. The . is the member of operator when it appears anywhere but in a numeric floating-point constant, where it separates the whole part from the fraction.

owner   The UNIX user who has control over a file's access modes, who pays for its storage, and so on. The UNIX system's ownership mechanism starts with a user id number, which appears in each person's entry in the '/etc/passwd' file. Each time a user creates or acquires a file, that person's user id number is recorded in the file's i-node. The long format listing of the `ls` command lists file owners; when an owner cannot be found in the password file the user id number is listed instead. Most of the files owned by individual users reside in their personal subtree.

P

page layout The appearance of a page of a document. Important aspects of page layout are the margins, the page headings, and the page footers.

page offset The distance of a document's left margin from the left edge of the paper.

paginate To divide a text file into pages, usually so files will be more attractive when printed. The UNIX program `pr` paginates files; it also can add headers and footers, page numbers, and make other simple format adjustments. UNIX also contains programs for displaying a file in screen-sized pages. *See also* screen pager.

paging A memory management technique that allows unused portions of a program to be stored temporarily on disk to make room for more urgently needed information in main memory. Paging is similar to swapping, except that paging does not copy an entire process out to disk; rather, it copies just the least needed part of process to disk. Only computers with sophisticated memory management hardware can support paging, while any computer hardware architecture can support swapping. One of the key features of a computer system with paging is that programs that are too large to fit into main memory can run. This capability is absent in systems that don't support paging. *See also* swapping.

panic To react to an unmanageable situation as gracefully as possible. Several UNIX programs panic when intolerable errors occur, but the best known panics are those of the UNIX kernel. It will panic in certain cases of hardware malfunction, or when it runs out of key resources, such as swap space.

parallel communication   Communication in which all the bits in an entire byte or word are transmitted simultaneously, unlike a serial communication link, in which each bit is transmitted sequentially. Parallel communication systems can be very fast, but the hardware costs are usually larger than for serial communication systems. Parallel communication is mostly used to connect equipment that is physically close. Printers are often connected to computers via a parallel connection.

parameter substitution   The shell's replacement of a reference to a variable or parameter by its value. Also called *variable substitution.* For example, the following dialogue displays the current setting of the $TERM variable.

```
$ echo $TERM
ansi
$ _
```

When the shell reads in the echo command line, it notices that the word *$TERM* starts with a currency symbol, which means that it is a reference to a variable. The shell then looks up the value of the $TERM variable in its list of variables and values. Finally the shell executes the echo command with the argument ansi, and the echo command does what it always does: outputs its command line arguments to the standard output.

parent directory   Directory immediately above the current directory. In the UNIX system, the filename '..' (dot dot) in the current directory is always a synonym for the parent directory. Unless you are in the root directory, you can cd to the parent directory by issuing the command cd .. .

parenthesis

Either of the symbols (or) that is often used to indicate grouping.

In the Bourne and C shells, a set of commands surrounded by parentheses will be performed by a subshell, not by the current shell.

In C, parentheses are used to control grouping in expressions and declarations, to surround type names in type casts, and to surround function argument lists.

parent process   A process that has initiated child processes, using the fork system call. Each process can always identify its parent because the parent process id number is recorded in the process' user table. *See also* fork.

parse   To understand the structure, and sometimes the meaning, of a grammar. The term is often applied to software, such as the compiler, that analyze and convert their input. Parsing is primarily concerned with examining and classifying the high-level objects in a program, such as expressions and statements. Parsing is often a recursive, or self-referential, process. The UNIX system has the yacc program, which is an aid for writing programs that parse their input. *See also* lexical analysis.

parser   A program (or a part of a program) that parses.

partition

A region of a disk that contains a filesystem. *See* filesystem layout.

To create disk partitions, therby making a large disk easier to manage.

Pascal   A high-level language developed by Niklaus Wirth for teaching programming. It has more type checking and other safety features than does the C language but is generally acknowledged to be less powerful than C. Pascal is available in most Berkeley versions of UNIX and is widely used as a teaching language.

password   A personal code that validates an individual's identity, or a code that is used when a file is encrypted. In the UNIX system, the password must be entered during each login. The UNIX system disables input echoing during password entry, so that passwords remain more private. Good passwords are memorable; they should not be too short (many systems require at least six characters); they should not be common names, they should not be words found in the dictionary; and they should not be telephone numbers, addresses, birthdates, social security numbers, and the like. Unfortunately, passwords are often chosen to be the name of a spouse, child, or close friend; this invites trouble.

password encryption   The process of encrypting a password. In the UNIX system, passwords are not stored in ordinary clear text form because they could be too easily compromised. Instead passwords are stored in an encrypted form. When you enter your password during the login procedure, it is encrypted, and then the result of the encryption is compared with the encrypted password stored in the '/etc/passwd' file. If the two match, the login continues, but if they are different, then the login procedure returns to the password entry phase.

password file   A file that contains passwords and other information about users. On the UNIX system, the password file is called '/etc/passwd'. Each line of '/etc/passwd' contains information that is used during the login process, including the user's login name, the encrypted password, the user id number, the group id number, the name of the home directory, and the name of the login shell. Each time a user attempts to log in, the password entered during the login process is encrypted and compared with the password stored in the password file. If they match, then the login session commences, using the specified home directory, login shell, user id number, and group id number.

password stealer   A program that is designed to dupe you into revealing your password. Usually the program is left running on a terminal in a university computer center. It prompts you to enter your login name and password. When that is accomplished, the program stores the information in a secret file, informs you that your login is incorrect, and then exits, thereby allowing the real login program to take over. Be suspicious if you correctly enter your password, yet fail to gain access to the system. Change your password, and report the problem to the system administrator. *See also* security.

$PATH   A shell variable that contains the current search string. Each time you ask the shell to execute a command, it looks in each directory mentioned in the $PATH search string. If found, the command is executed. Otherwise, the shell complains that it cannot find the command. (This procedure is slightly different in modern Bourne shells, the Korn shell, and the C shell.) The individual directory names in $PATH are separated by colons. A pair of interior colons, or leading or trailing colons, signify the current directory. The $PATH for the root account should never mention the current directory because of security concerns. The following example demonstrates the importance of the $PATH variable.

```
$ ulfix chap8.t
sh: ulfix: not found
$ ls /usr1/kc/bin/ulfix
ulfix
$ echo $PATH
/bin:/usr/bin:/usr/ucb:/usr/local/bin
$ PATH=$PATH:/usr1/kc/bin
$ echo $PATH
/bin:/usr/bin:/usr/ucb:/usr/local/bin:/usr1/kc/bin
$ ulfix chap8.t
$ _
```

See also Trojan horse; path, search.

pathname   A route through the filesystem that leads to a file. A pathname consists of a list of directory names separated by / characters plus a final filename. There are two kinds of pathnames: *relative* pathnames and *absolute* pathnames. Relative pathnames start in the current directory, while absolute pathnames start in the root directory. The first character is an absolute pathname is always /, which, when used at the beginning of a pathname, refers to the root directory. Paths can ascend the filesystem hierarchy by mentioning the name '..', which leads to the parent of a given directory; all other components of a pathname descend the filesystem. For example, the pathname '/usr/bin/lex' is an absolute pathname; it specifies a path that starts in the root directory, leads to the 'usr' directory, then to the 'bin' directory, and finally to the file 'lex'. Another example is the relative pathname '../bin/ulfix', which ascends from the current directory to the parent, and then descends from there to the 'bin' directory, and from there to the 'ulfix' file. *See also* absolute pathname; relative pathname; filename.

path, search   The list of directories where the shell attempts to access the commands that you enter. It is stored in the $PATH shell variable. *See also* $PATH.

pattern space   The sed edit buffer. It usually holds just the current line of the input. *See also* sed.

PCC   *See* portable C compiler.

PDP-11   A computer manufactured by the Digital Equipment Corporation, which was important during the early development of the UNIX system.

peripheral device   Hardware that is electrically, and sometimes physically, connected to a computer. Peripheral devices usually perform I/O operations. Complex peripheral devices (also called *peripherals*), such as large disk drives, are often connected to a controller, which manages the transfer of data between the peripheral and the computer's memory. *See also* interface; controller.

permissions   Access modes associated with a file. *See* file access mode; directory access mode.

permuted index   A feature of the traditional UNIX manual that makes it easier to locate topics. For example you can look up the word *move* in the center column of the permuted manual to see which citations in the UNIX manual have a brief description containing the word *move*. Similar to a keyword in context index.

per process data segment   *See* user table.

personal computer   A computer designed to be used by an individual. Typical personal computers have a graphics display, disk, processor, and memory. Some personal computers run multitasking operating systems such as the UNIX system, while others run simpler systems such as MS-DOS. Some people use the term personal computer more narrowly, meaning a personal computer manufactured by IBM, or one of the computers that is functionally identical to those made by IBM.

pic   An `nroff`/`troff` preprocessor that makes it easier to typeset simple line drawings and charts. *See also* `troff`.

pica   A unit of typographic measurement, equal to a sixth of an inch.

pid   *See* process identification number.

pipe

Connection between the standard output of one program and the standard input of another program. The command line symbol for a pipe connection is | (vertical bar). Also called a pipe connection. For example, the following dialogue shows a pipe between the `ls` command and the `wc` command.

```
$ ls | wc -l
12
$ _
```

The word count command (`wc -l`) counts the lines of its input. Its output message, 12, says that it received 12 lines from `ls`, indicating that there are 12 files in the current directory.

To route data from the standard output of one process into the standard input of another, using a UNIX pipe connection.

pipe connection   An I/O connection that is created by the `pipe` system call. A pipe connection sends data to (or acquires data from) another process, not a file.

pipe fitting   *See* pipe connection.

pipeline   Group of commands joined by pipe connections. Commands in a pipeline are performed simultaneously, with the output from each command serving as input for the subsequent command. (This is distinct from a simple sequence of commands joined by semicolons, where the commands are performed in order, but without being linked through I/O redirection.) *See also* I/O redirection; standard I/O connections.

pitch   The number of characters per inch in a monospace type-face. Typewriters often operate at 10- or 12-pitch, which means 10 or 12 characters per inch.

pixel   An abbreviation derived from the term *picture element*. A pixel is an individually addressable element of the display grid of a raster graphics device. *See also* raster graphics.

point   A unit of typographic measure, equal to 1/72 inch. The size of a typeface is often specified in points. Ten points is a common size. A 72-point typeface is 1 inch tall.

pointer   A data type that holds the address of a location in memory. C has more facilities and operators for pointers than most other languages.

pointer arithmetic   Any of the three arithmetic operations that C allows on pointers: adding a numeric value to a pointer, subtracting a numeric value from a pointer, or subtracting two pointers. So that C pointers work analogously with arrays, addition of (and subtraction of) a numeric value *n* to a pointer makes that pointer point toward the *n*th item in the sequence. Similarly, the result of subtracting two pointers is the number of elements that separate them (the two pointers must point at the same type, and the comparison doesn't make sense unless the two pointers are pointing into the same array).

point size   The size of a typeface, measured in points.

pop   To remove the most recently entered item from a stack. *See also* push.

port   To move a software system to a new environment. Some examples are: to adapt a version of UNIX for one computer system to run on another computer system; to modify a program written for Berkeley UNIX so that it runs on a System V system; to rewrite sections of a UNIX program so that it runs on an MS-DOS system.

portable   A software system that can be modified to run in a different environment. *See also* port; machine independent.

portable C compiler   A C compiler written by Stephen Johnson in such a way that it is relatively easy to adapt the C compiler to run on different computer architectures. The portable C compiler is an important tool for moving UNIX and C to new environments.

portable C I/O library   A set of I/O routines that are available for all versions of C. These routines are based on the idea of a stream, which is similar to the concept that underlies Pascal I/O. All I/O operations are locally buffered, so that I/O requests are only made to the operating system when local buffers are full or empty. Some of the major routines are getc and putc (single character I/O), gets and puts (line by line I/O), fprintf and fscanf (formatted I/O), fread and fwrite (block I/O), and fopen and fclose (file opening and closing). It was first implemented on UNIX machines. Also called the standard I/O library. *See also* buffered I/O.

postfix   An operator that comes after its operand.

postprocessor   A processor that performs final processing on data.

PostScript   A page description (layout) language developed by Adobe, Inc. It is a common standard for sending information to laser printers and typesetters, and it is also used as the basis for a graphics interface on graphic workstations, much like X windows.

#pragma   An ANSI C preprocessor feature that allows compiler-specific directives to be inserted into a program. #pragma directives are often used to specify code generation options.

precedence   The binding strength of an arithmetic or logical operator. For example, most people are accustomed to interpreting the expression 5 + 2 * 10 to mean multiply 2 times 10, and then add 5, resulting in 25. A different result is obtained when the addition is performed first. Thus, in common expressions, multiplication has precedence over addition. In computer languages it is important to clearly establish a precedence for every operator, so that there is no ambiguity. When operators in a programming language are defined to have the same precedence, then operations are specified to occur from left to right or from right to left.

prefix   An operator that precedes its operand.

preprocess   To perform an preliminary processing on input data. *See also* preprocessor.

preprocessor   A program that performs preliminary processing on input data. In the UNIX system, the C preprocessor is the first stage of the C language compiler. It performs file inclusion, simple macro replacement, and conditional code inclusion.

preventive maintenance   Performing standard maintenance on equipment, in the hopes that such maintenance will prevent future equipment failures. Typical tasks are cleaning, visual inspection, making measurements and adjustments, and replacing consumable parts such as filters and belts.

primary store   *See* main memory.

primitives   Lowest-level operations in a system. In the C language, the primitives are arithmetic and logical operations on data. In the shell programming language, the primitives are the operations of the UNIX commands.

printf   A C subroutine for formatted output. printf can convert values into text format so that they can be printed or displayed. The format of the output is controlled by a conversion specification string.

printing terminal   A computer terminal that uses a print mechanism for output, plus a keyboard for input. Also called a *hard-copy terminal. See also* teletype.

priority   A number associated with a process that the kernel's scheduler uses when determining which process should execute next. Processes with high priorities (lower priority numbers) get larger and/or more frequent time slices. While executing, a process' priority falls; while waiting for I/O a process' priority rises. A user can introduce a bias into the scheduler's calculations using the nice command. Ordinary users can only lower their own process' priorities, whereas the superuser can lower or raise any process' priorities. *See also* scheduler.

privilege   *See* file access mode; directory access mode.

procedure   A group of statements or commands that are called (activated) as a group. In most programming languages, procedures can have local variables, can be passed arguments, and can return a value. Often the term *procedure* is used for routines that do not return a value and the term *function* is used for those that do return a value. *See also* function.

process

A program that is being executed on a UNIX system. When a program, such as vi, is simultaneously being executed by several people, there are several processes, but only one program. Each process is catalogued in the system's process table.

To manipulate data.

process group   A group of related processes. Typically, all of a user's processes that result from a single login session are members of one process group. Process groups are important because software signals generated by keyboard characters are sent to all the members of the current process group. It is also possible for a daemon process to detach itself from its original process group and to become a member of another process group. The default mechanism for establishing a process group is for a process (usually getty) to be the first to open a communication line. When this happens, the tty driver uses the process identification number as the process group number. Offspring of the original process all continue to be members of this process group.

process identification number   A unique number assigned by the UNIX system kernel to identify each process. Often called a *pid*. The pid numbers for current processes can be printed by the ps command. When a program is submitted for background processing, the shell automatically displays its pid number on the user's terminal. You must know a process' pid number to send it a signal using the kill command.

process image   *See* program image.

process one   init, which is the second process created by UNIX when booting. *See also* init.

process status   The current description of a UNIX process. This includes information such as the process' state (running, waiting for I/O, swapped out, etc.), its priority, its real (and effective) user and group id number, and its cumulative execution time. Such information is displayed by the ps command.

process table   A data structure in the UNIX kernel that catalogs the current processes. It contains information about their size, location, priority, received signals, and so forth. The number of entries in the process table is an absolute cap on the number of processes that a UNIX system can manage simultaneously. Information from the process table is displayed and formatted using the ps command. *See also* data structure.

process zero   The first process created by UNIX when booting. Process zero is said to be executing when the kernel is scheduling other tasks.

processor   *See* CPU.

profiling   Running a program in such a way that it can be analyzed to determine where it spends most of its time. Profiling is useful when you want to optimize a program because it identifies the critical regions, where most programs spend the majority of their time. UNIX contains several programs for profiling software, including prof and gprof.

program

A sequence of instructions that can cause the machine to perform some function. Programs are written in many ways and in many languages. There are two main program types on UNIX systems: programs that are compiled to machine language instructions, and programs that are executed indirectly by a software-based interpreter. The C language is an example of a language that is usually compiled, and the shell programming language is an example of an interpretive language. Some languages, such as Pascal, may be either interpreted or compiled. A program is the creation; when it is executing in a UNIX machine, it becomes a process.

To create a computer program.

program generator   A program that can create software. They are commonly applied to tasks that are standardized and well understood, yet tasks that are difficult for people to program. The UNIX system has two standard program generators: yacc, which can create parser routines; and lex, which can create lexical analysis routines. Both yacc and lex read as input a tabular description of the task.

program image   A version of a program in a form that corresponds directly to a given computer's hardware. Program images are contained in binary executable files and in core dump files.

programmable read-only memory (PROM)   A form of read-only memory that can be loaded with values (programmed) after it leaves the factory, usually by engineers using specialized equipment. *See also* read/write memory; ultraviolet eraseable programmable read-only memory.

Programmer's Workbench   A set of tools and facilities developed under UNIX to make it easier to develop software.

programming language   Body of instructions usable for directing the activity of a computer. Some of the most common languages on UNIX systems are: the various shells, for automating tasks that can be performed by UNIX utility programs; C, for writing new utility programs; Fortran, for scientific and numerical programs; Pascal, for learning to program; and Lisp, for AI programs. Numerous other programming languages are available for UNIX systems.

PROM   *See* programmable read-only memory.

prompt

Message printed by a program to indicate that the program is ready to accept a command from the user. The primary prompt for the Bourne shell can be changed by assigning a value to the variable

$PS1. On most systems the default shell prompts are a sharp (#) for the superuser, a percent sign (%) for C shell users, and a currency symbol ($) for Bourne shell users.

To display a prompt.

protocol   Standard method for performing a task. Communication protocols, such as the UUCP protocol, enable systems to communicate in a mutually agreed-on manner.

$PS1   A Bourne shell variable that contains the value of the primary prompt string. You can change your prompt by changing this variable.

```
$ echo The prompt is $PS1
The prompt is $
$ PS1="Yes, boss "
Yes, boss PS1=osh- /bin/osh
osh-
ps -x
 PID TT STAT  TIME COMMAND
 1812 03 S    0:00 -sh
 (sh)
 2908 03 S    0:01 -sh (osh)
 2918 03 R    0:03 ps x
osh- exit
Yes, boss _
```

$PS2   The Bourne shell's secondary prompt. It uses this prompt when commands are obviously incomplete.

```
$ echo secondary prompt $PS2
secondary prompt >
$ echo "Hello Mr. Phelps.
> Today your assignment is to
> . . .
> will disavow any knowledge of your activities."
Hello Mr. Phelps.
Today your assignment is to
 . . .
will disavow any knowledge of your activities.
$ _
```

pseudo-tty   A UNIX special device that appears, to a program, like an ordinary tty file, but is actually a communication endpoint.

pseudonym   *See* link.

pty   *See* pseudo-tty.

pure executable   A program whose text segment (the machine language instructions) is sharable among several processes. Pure executable programs are advantageous for programs such as the shell that are likely to be executed by several users simultaneously. When several people are all executing the same pure executable program, there is one copy of the program text (instructions) in memory, plus several copies of the program data in memory, one for each user. The term *pure* derives from the method used to link a pure executable. When the linker is creating a pure executable, it places instructions into one memory region, separate from the three regions whose content changes while a process executes: data, BSS, and stack. Thus the text region is said to be pure because it only contains text. If the text contained anything that changed during execution, each process would need a private copy. But because a pure executable's text just contains (constant) instructions, all processes can share a single copy. The file command differentiates between pure executable programs and ordinary executable programs.

push   To place something onto a stack. *See also* pop.

pwd   A UNIX command that prints the name of the current directory. *See also* directory, current; cd.

Q

queue   Ordered list of jobs, each awaiting its turn, typically for execution or printing. *See also* spooler.

quit character   A keyboard character that you can type to cause most software to terminate, with a core dump. Except for causing a core dump, the quit character is similar to the interrupt character. Striking the quit character send the SIGQUIT signal (3) to your process.

quit signal   A signal (3) that is sent to a process to cause it to terminate and dump core, usually so that it can be debugged.

quotes   Characters that surround (or precede) an item of text, usually to indicate a grouping or altered meaning. The Bourne shell has three quotes: double quotes (" ... ") to weakly quote the enclosed text, single quotes (´ ... ´) to strongly quote the enclosed text, and the backslash (\) to quote the following character. *See also* quoting.

quotes, C   The C programming language has two forms of quotes: double quotes for strings and single quotes for single characters. The following C declarations create single character variables c_1 and c_2 initialized to *a* and *z*, respectively, and a character string msg1 initialized to *Enter cmd->*.

```
char c1 = 'a';
char c2 = 'z';
char msg1[] = "Enter cmd->";
```

quoting   Preventing metacharacters (such as the shell's *, etc.) and other special characters (such as white space or newlines) from having their special meanings, often by surrounding them with quotation marks. The shell has three forms of quotes: double quotes, which are a weak form of quoting; single quotes, which are stronger; and the backslash, which quotes the immediately following character. Within double quotes, parameter and command substitution occur. Thus $ and ` are magic within double quotes. Within single quotes all special characters lose their meaning. A backslash removes the meaning from the following character, and the character sequence \<NL> vanishes. The following dialogue demonstrates the Bourne shell's three forms of quoting:

```
$ echo *.c
hist.c   calc.c   rast.c   conf.c
$ echo "*.c"
*.c
$ echo $TERM
ansi
$ echo "$TERM"
ansi
$ echo '$TERM'
$TERM
$ echo \$TERM
$TERM
$ echo he\
llo
hello
$ _
```

R

radix   The number on which a number system is based. Most computers operate internally using a radix of two (binary). Programmers often refer to computer addresses and constants using the more compact octal or hexadecimal radices. Most people are more familiar with the radix of ten, which is the basis of the Arabic number system.

RAM (Random-access memory)   Memory in which any location can be accessed quickly. Although fast access to any location is also a characteristic of PROM and ROM memory, the term *RAM* is usually used to refer to memory that can be both read and written. RAM is used as the main memory of most computers. Perhaps because it is more pronounceable, this term has replaced the acronym RWM (read/write memory).

raster   A series of parallel lines. The term usually refers to the lines drawn by a video disply or by a printer to create an image. Each line is divided into short segments called *pixels* (picture elements) whose intensity is individually controlled. *See also* pixel; raster graphics.

raster graphics   Images created from a grid of picture elements. Most video displays, and most dot matrix printers, are raster graphics devices. In some raster graphics devices it is possible to assign different intensities or colors to each picture element (pixel). The term *raster* derives from television technology. In an ordinary television the electron beam that illuminates the screen is moved across the screen one line at a time; a complete set of these lines is called a *raster*. *See also* pixel; BITBLT.

Ratfor   A programming language. A Ratfor compiler translates a Ratfor source program into Fortran source, and then a Fortran compiler performs the remainder of the translation. The advantage of

Ratfor is that it creates a more productive and easier to read user programming language, while retaining the numerical qualities and universality of the Fortran language. Ratfor is available on most UNIX systems that support Fortran. The word *Ratfor* is derived from the term *rational Fortran. See also Fortran.*

raw mode　A state of the UNIX tty handler, in which individual characters are made available to applications programs as soon as they are typed. This is in contrast to the usual mode of the tty handler, which gives characters to applications programs only when a complete line has been typed. In raw mode the usual erase, kill and interrupt keyboard characters are not special; when these characters are typed their ASCII codes are simply passed to the program. The term *raw* describes the lack of processing of user input by the tty handler. *See also* cbreak mode; cooked mode.

rc　A term that is often used in UNIX systems to denote an initialization script. The term may have derived from the phrase run commands. The original rc script is '/etc/rc', which is the script that is executed when the system boots. Others include '.cshrc' (C shell initialization scripts) and '.exrc' (ex/vi initialization scripts).

RCS (revision control system)　A software system, similar in function to SCCS, that helps to maintain and document versions of text files.

read　To acquire data, usually from a file or I/O device.

read-only memory (ROM)　A memory element whose information can be read but not altered (written). ROMs often contain firmware that provides basic, hardware-dependent services. There are two basic types of ROMs: PROMs, which can be loaded with values (programmed) by engineers using special (but inexpensive) equipment, and factory mask ROMs, which can only be programmed at the factory during manufacture. In large-volume applications, the factory mask ROMs are much less expensive than PROMs, but PROMs are much more flexible because they can be programmed individually.

read permission   Permission for a user's process to read data from a certain file during the execution of a program or command. *See also* file access mode; directory access mode.

real time   Occurring in the computer at about the same time as an external event and keeping pace with that event. Typical real-time tasks are collecting experimental data at a certain rate, or periodically updating a graphics display.

reassign

To redefine the meaning of a key on the keyboard. For example, the <Ctrl-C> code is often used as the interrupt character, but the stty program can reassign the interrupt function to another key code, such as <DEL>.

To change the value of a variable.

record

One complete description in a database file. Records are composed of fields. In many text format database files, such as the '/etc/passwd' file, a record is one line of the file. In other format files, such as the '/etc/termcap' terminal characteristics database, records may span more than one line of the file. The grep program can extract individual records (lines) from text format files that have single line records. *See also* field; array.

To store a piece of information. For example, the login program records login information in the '/etc/utmp' and '/etc/wtmp' files.

record locking   A capability of many systems that allows individual records in a file to be marked as busy by one process, so that they cannot be accessed by another process. This prevents two separate processes from simultaneously reading a particular record, making changes to the record, and then writing in back into the file, thereby losing one of the process's changes. Record locking (or file locking) is important in multitasking database systems because it synchronizes access to the data. Record locking is a finer grained mechanism than file locking. *See also* file locking.

record separator   A character or character sequence that separates the records in a file. The most common record separator in the UNIX system is the newline character. An example of a program that uses a different record separator is `refer`, which separates records with pairs of newlines.

recover

To retrieve the contents of a file from a backup or from an archive.

To try to react appropriately to adverse circumstances. For example, the uucp software tries to recover from errors induced by noisy phone lines by retransmission.

recursion   A computer programming technique, whereby software invokes itself. Often used to solve problems that can easily be described with a self-referential definition. For example, the common definition of the Fibonacci number sequence, $f_0 = 0$, $f_1 = 1$, and $f_{n>1} = f_{n-2} + f_{n-1}$, is self-referential. A limiting condition must exist, or the software will never complete.

recursion, direct   A form of recursion in which a routine calls itself.

recursion, indirect   A form of recursion in which a routine calls some other routine (or routines), which then calls the original routine.

recursive   A software routine that invokes itself (direct recursion) or a software routine that invokes some other routine that in turn invokes the original routine (indirect recursion).

redirection   *See* I/O redirection.

refer   An `nroff/troff` preprocessor that makes it easier to typeset references. *See also* `troff`.

register   A CPU storage location that can be accessed very rapidly. In most computers, frequently used data elements are moved from memory into registers so that they may be accessed more rapidly. Most computers contain only a small number of registers, although some computer designs contain hundreds of registers.

register (storage class)   In C, a derivative of the auto storage class. The intent is to allow the programmer to point out frequently used variables so that the compiler can place them into the most accessible storage, which is usually a hardware register. Because of hardware and software limitations, the compiler is not always able to fulfill the request. In this case, register variables are treated as auto variables. It is not permissible to take the address of a register variable.

regular expression   A sequence of characters and/or metacharacters that can match a set of fixed text strings. In UNIX, the most common elements of regular expressions are ordinary characters, which match themselves; characters enclosed in square brackets, which match any one of the enclosed characters; a period, which matches any single character; and an asterisk, which matches zero or more occurrences of the preceding single character regular expression. Thus the regular expression [smbhdcl]ad can match any of the following: sad, mad, bad, had, dad, cad, and lad. Regular expressions are used in many UNIX utilities, including ed, ex/vi, grep, sed, and awk.

rehash   To recompute a hash table. The C shell maintains a hash table for all the commands accessible by your search path. If new commands are installed in an executable directory while a C shell is running, they will not be easily accessible until you execute the C shell built-in command rehash to update the hash table. *See also* hash.

relative pathname   A pathname that starts in the current directory (in contrast to an absolute pathname, which starts in the root directory). For example, the relative pathname '../video/vidsubs/cursor.c' starts in the current directory, ascends to the parent directory, descends from there to the video directory, and then descends further to the vidsubs directory, leading finally to the 'cursor.c' file. *See also* pathname; absolute pathname.

remote procedure call   A network mechanism that allows a program on one system to make a procedure call on another system.

request (nroff/troff)   An nroff/troff command, such as .sp, which is a request for extra vertical space.

restore   To recover archival or backup data, often by using the UNIX restore program.

restricted constant expression   *See* constant expression, restricted.

return   *See* carriage return; return statement.

return statement   A statement in many programming languages that signifies the completion of a procedure and that causes the flow of control to return to the point from which the procedure was called.

RFS   A System V networking standard that allows processes on one machine to access files on another machine via a network.

Richards, Martin   Designer of BCPL, a systems programming language.

Ritchie, Dennis M.   The originator of C and the coinventor (with Ken Thompson) of the UNIX system.

roff   An obsolete UNIX text formatter. Some of the style of the troff formatter is derived from roff. The name comes from the phrase *run off*, which is an even older text formatter and also a description of the process of printing a document.

ROM   *See* read-only memory.

root

The base directory of the UNIX filesystem. *See* directory, root.

The login name for the UNIX superuser. To acquire superuser privileges, one must either log in using the login name *root* or execute the su command. In either case, the next step is to enter the root password, to convince the system that you are an authorized superuser.

root directory   *See* directory, root.

root filesystem   The filesystem that is immediately available when the system is first booted. The root filesystem is not mounted using the /etc/mount program, and it cannot be unmounted by running the /etc/umount program. (Some specialized UNIX systems have been modified to allow removable root filesystems.) When the UNIX system boots up to single user mode, only the programs and files in the root filesystem are available, until the /etc/mount program is run to mount more filesystems.

root login   The UNIX superuser's account. This account can be accessed using the login name *root* or by using the su command. In either case, you must enter the root password correctly before the system will permit access to the account.

route

A path in a network.

To pick a path through a network, and then send messages along that path.

routine   *See* program; subroutine; function.

RS-232 (also RS-232C)   An industry standard for connecting computers to peripherals, such as modems, printers, and terminals. The RS-232 system uses serial data transfer over a pair of wires, but there are also several control signals on additional wires. Many RS-232 capabilities are designed to connect modems to a computer, and some of these capabilities are not necessary when connecting printers or terminals to a computer. Full RS-232 conformance usually requires a 25-wire connection between devices, but many devices operate successfully with 15-wire connections, with 7-wire connections, or with the minimum of 3 wires.

RTFM   A polite term used by system managers (and USENET gurus) to ask a user to please read the manual.

run   *See* execute.

runtime   The period of time that a program is running. "I was able to compile the program successfully, but it always failed at runtime."

runtime library   A collection of software modules that a programmer can incorporate into a program. The library services are provided while the program is running, hence the term. The C language assumes the presence of a runtime library because the basic functionality that is built into the compiler does not provide for many essential operations, such as I/O, an operating system interface, and mathematics support.

rvalue   A value that can appear on the right-hand side of an assignment statement. rvalues do not have to indicate a place for a value to be stored. In C, rvalues can be constants, functions, and arrays, plus all of the things that can be lvalues. *See also* lvalue.

S

save text bit   The bit in the file access variable in each i-node that enables/disables the save text mode. Also called the save text bit. *See* save text mode; file access mode.

save text mode   A mode for binary executable files that causes them to remain in swap space even when they are not being executed. Save text programs are best understood by comparison with ordinary executable programs. When ordinary executable programs are not being executed, their text is not present in memory or swap space; the only copy of the program is in the original disk file. However, save text executables are kept resident, either in memory or in swap space, from their first usage until the system is shutdown. The advantage is that files in swap space are stored contiguously, and systems are often configured to minimize disk drive latency when accessing swap space. Thus it is faster to load a program from swap space than from the filesystem. The disadvantage is that swap space is a precious resource, and giving the save text mode to too many programs can reduce your swap space operating margin. The UNIX superuser is the only user who can assign the sticky mode to a file. If save text mode is used at all, it is generally assigned to heavily used programs such as the vi text editor. The save text mode is indicated in a long format ls listing by the character *t* in place of the other's execute privilege. Also called the *sticky mode* because the program gets stuck in swap space. The save text mode was more important in the early days of UNIX, when disks and filesystems had lower performance than is common on modern systems. *See also* swap space; file access mode.

scalar type   A data type that consists of an ordered set of values.

scalar processor   A hardware device that can accelerate a machine's scalar arithmetic performance.

scanf   A C function for managing formatted input. scanf converts the values in its input text into binary values that are stored in ordinary variables. The conversions are controlled by a specification string. The operation is the complement of that performed by printf, and the syntax of the conversion specification string is similar to printf.

SCCS   The Source Code Control System. A UNIX subsystem that makes it possible to retrieve old or variant versions of a text file. Often used in large programming projects to provide an audit trail and to make it possible to undo inappropriate software modifications. *See also* RCS.

scheduler   The part of the UNIX kernel that schedules processes for execution. *See also* priority.

scheduling   Selecting a process for execution in a time-sharing system.

scope rules   In a programming language, a set of rules that determine the visibility of identifiers. In C, variables declared within a function may have the same name as those declared externally. In such a case, references to that name inside the function access the local variable, other accesses in the program access the external variables. For example, in the following program function a accesses its own min but function b accesses the external min.

```
int min = 2;
void main()
{
     a();
     b();
}
void a()
{
     int min = 1;
     printf("%d\n", min);    /* the local min */
}
void b()
{
     printf("%d\n", min);    /* the external min */
}
```

The output of this program is a *1* and then a *2*. There are also several different classes of identifier, each with its own scope. For example, structure tags, and structure variables are in separate scopes, and the members of each structure are in their own scope. Thus the following structure definition is possible.

```
struct max {
     int max;
} max;
```

The first max is the structure tag, the second is the structure's member, and the third refers to the whole structure. This definition is possible because each *max* is in a different scope.

screen editor   *See* visual editor.

screen pager   A program that lets you view a text file, one screenful (page) at a time, on your terminal. Berkeley UNIX systems contain the more screen pager and System V contains the pg screen pager. The traditional program for paginating a file prior to printing is pr. *See also* paginate.

Scribe   A text formatter developed by Brian Reid.

script   A text file containing commands, often shell or editor commands. Although the term *script* and the term *shell program* are often used interchangeably, the term *script* often is used to describe something that is simpler than a shell program. *See also* shell program.

scroll

Traditional: adding a new line of information at the bottom of the screen, causing everything else on the screen to move up one line.

To move information up or down (or sometimes left or right) on the screen.

sdb   A symbolic System V debugger.

search path   *See* search string.

search string   List of directories for the shell to search when executing each entered command. The search string usually includes the user's current directory, the '/bin' directory, and the '/usr/bin' directory. The search string can be altered by assigning a new value to the variable $PATH. Also called *search path*.

secondary prompt   The prompt that the Bourne shell displays after you have entered part of an obviously incomplete command. Some examples of obviously incomplete commands are unfinished structured commands, such as for or while loops, here documents, and commands that contain unterminated quotations. The value of the secondary prompt is stored in the $PS2 shell variable.

secondary store   *See* mass storage device.

security   Safeguards that have been employed to protect the operational integrity of a system and to protect the privacy of the information on that system. The UNIX system is a moderately secure computer system. It can withstand most casual probes, but it has several well-known weaknesses that can be used to advantage by those who are determined to breach the system. *See also* Trojan horse; password stealer.

sed   The UNIX stream editor. sed modifies its input text according to a script. *See also* stream editor.

seek   To change the read/write location. In a disk system, a seek is a movement of the read/write head from one place to another. In a program, a seek is a repositioning of the read or write location in a file. Seeks typically move the read or write location to an absolute position in the file, a position at some distance from the current position, or to the end of the file. Seeks are only possible with ordinary files. It is not possible to seek on a pipe connection, or a connection to a terminal. The UNIX system contains the lseek system call, and the C standard I/O library has the fseek subroutine.

semantic error   A programming error that results in a syntactically correct program that does not perform the intended operation. For example, a sorting program that orders the input incorrectly must contain a semantic error. Semantic errors are usually impossible for a compiler or interpreter to diagnose; instead, the programmer must find the problem and design a solution. *See also* syntax error.

semiconductor   A material that has a conductivity between that of good conductors, such as metals, and that of insulators. Semiconductors are the basis of modern electronic circuit technology.

sequential evaluation operator   *See* operator, comma.

serial communication   Sending data as a sequence of bits, as on a RS-232 communication line or an Ethernet. *See also* modem; direct connection; parallel communication.

server   *See* network server.

session   Interactive use of the computer between login and logout. In the UNIX system, one person can engage in several sessions simultaneously, using multiple terminals or using several windows on a multiwindow terminal. Also called a *login session.*

set gid mode   *See* set group id mode.

set group id mode   A file access mode that lets one run a program using the privileges of the executable program file's group, rather than the group privileges of the person running the program.

163

This capability is used so that a user running a program can access files to which that person would otherwise be denied access. The set user id mode is displayed as a *s* in place of the group execute privilege in a long format `ls` listing. It can be assigned to a file by the file's owner by the `chmod` program. *See also* set user id mode; file access mode; group id number.

set uid mode   *See* set uid mode.

set user id mode   A file access mode that lets one run a program using the privileges of the executable program file's owner, rather than the privileges of the person running the program. This capability is used so that a person running a program can access files to which that person would otherwise be denied access. For example, the creator of a game program might place a list of clues in a personally owned file that is only readable by owner. Such a file access mode would normally prevent others from reading the file. However, if the game program executable file has the set user id mode, then anyone running the game program can access the clues file (but only as dictated by the program logic). The set user id mode is displayed as a *s* in place of the user execute privilege in a long format `ls` listing. It can be assigned to a file by the file's owner by the `chmod` program. *See also* set user id mode; file access mode; user id number.

Seventh Edition   *See* Version 7.

shar file   A UNIX shell script that contains a group of files. When the shar file is interpreted by the shell, the files are extracted. The shar format is commonly used to mail files using standard mailers because the content of a shar file is exclusively text. Shar files are useful for sending groups of files to other UNIX systems, but most non-UNIX computer systems do not have software that can extract the contents of a shar file. The files in a shar script are embedded in shell here documents. Various utility programs exist to create shar files. The term comes from the phrase shell archive.

shared text   A capability of the UNIX system that allows multiple processes to share one copy of the program text. This makes the system more efficient, because it reduces the amount of memory and swap space that is required to run a given set of processes.

Programs that are commonly executed by more than one person at a time, such as the shell and the editor, often use shared text. Programs must be specially compiled to create a load image whose text can be shared.

shar file   *See* shar archive.

shell   A command/programming language that provides an interface to the UNIX operating system. As a command interpreter, the shell interactively accepts commands from users and arranges for the requested actions to occur. Its programming language features include flow control and string-valued variables. The two most common UNIX shells are the Bourne shell and the C shell. The term originates from the fact that the UNIX shell provides an environment for a computer user, somewhat like a seashell provides an environment for a sea animal. *See also* shell programming language; Bourne shell; C shell; Korn shell.

shell escape   A feature of many interactive UNIX programs that allows you to temporarily escape to a shell to enter shell commands. When your minisession with the shell is complete, you exit from the shell and return to your previous state in the interactive programs. Some UNIX programs that contain a shell escape are the text editors, the `mail` program, and the `write` program.

shell function   A shell function is analogous to a function in any other programming language; it is a group of statements that can be executed by name, can be passed arguments, and can return a value. Found in newer versions of the Bourne shell and all versions of the Korn shell.

shell program   A program written in the shell programming language. Shell programs are executed by a shell process that interprets their contents. Traditionally, shell programs are executed as follows. A shell program attempts to execute the program using the exec system call, once per directory in the search string. In each directory where the script is not found, the kernel returns the "file not found" error code. In the directory containing the script, the kernel refuses the request because the file does not start with the appropriate magic number for a binary executable, and it returns the "cannot execute" error code. Then the shell spawns a

165

subshell, with its input connected to the script. In Berkeley UNIX systems there is a special magic number, whose ASCII code is #!, that allows the kernel to recognize shell scripts. When the Berkeley kernel detects this code at the start of a script, it then uses the remainder of the line as the name of an interpreter to interpret the script. This Berkeley feature makes it easier for programs other than the shell to execute shell scripts. *See also* script; magic number.

shell programming language   The programming language that is implemented by the UNIX shell. There are two common UNIX shell programming languages: the Bourne shell language and the C shell language. Both are interpretive languages, that contain flow of control statements, the ability to execute UNIX utilities, I/O redirection, pipelines, and very simple facilities for managing variables. Shell programs are relatively quick and easy to develop, and many useful shell programs have been written by people whose primary job is something other than programming. The shell programming language is appropriate for writing programs that draw heavily on standard UNIX utility programs; it is inappropriate for programs that emphasize numeric manipulation, character manipulation, or that require high performance.

short-circuit evaluation   Evaluation of an expression only to the point at which the result is known. For example, in the expression a * b, the result of the expression can be determined without evaluating b if a is zero. However if b has side effects, short circuit evaluation will not yield the same program state as ordinary evaluation (it merely yields the same expression result). In C, logical expressions guarantee short circuit evaluation. *See also* operator, logical.

short data type   In C, an arithmetic data type that is the same size as, or smaller than, an integer. On thirty-two bit machines, a short is often 16 bits, while on 16 bit machines a short is often sixteen bits (as are integers).

side effects   In an expression, something that changes other than as a result of an assignment in an assignment statement. Some side effects are impossible to avoid. For example, an expression that calls an input routine alters the input file pointer. C has been widely criticized because many of its operators cause side effects. All the following C features can cause side effects and thus lead to unexpected results: the increment and decrement operators, the use of macros, the common practice of calling functions with pointers, and the common practice of using embedded assignment. For example, the following expression is nonportable because of its side effects: the increment of `ptr` in the right-hand expression. The operation is undefined (unpredictable) because there are no guarantees on the order in which the components of the expression are evaluated, but the result depends on when the side effect occurs.

```
int *ptr;
. . .
*ptr = *ptr++ + 10;
```

On a given machine, with a given compiler, the expression may (or may not) do what the programmer intended, but on different machines the operation may be different.

signal   A simple form of process to process communication on UNIX systems. When a process receives a signal, one of three things will happen: the process may ignore the signal, the process may be forced to terminate, or the process may execute an application-specific signal handler. Within a program, signals are sent to a process using the `kill` system call, and a process can manage incoming signals using the `signal` system call. At the user level, signals can be sent to a process using the `kill` command, in the Bourne shell the `trap` command is used to manage incoming signals, and in the C shell the `onintr` command is used to manage incoming signals. Arrived signals are recorded in the kernel's process table. Each time the kernel reactivates a process (i.e. after a period when the process has not been executing) it checks for new signals. If any have arrived, the appropriate action is taken. If the signal is nonfatal, then the process continues. *See also* interrupt signal; kill signal.

signal handler   A software routine that is activated automatically when a signal arrives. In C programs, signal handlers are installed using the `signal` system call; in Bourne shell programs, they are installed using the `trap` command; in C shell programs, they are installed using the `onintr` command.

signed   A C language keyword that indicates that the variable being declared should have both positive and negative values. Originally, all C integer data types (char, short, int, and long) were signed by default, and the unsigned keyword was used to make them unsigned. Modern compilers sometimes make characters unsigned by default (or they have an option that directs them to do so), and on such systems the signed keyword is necessary to create signed characters.

single-user   Pertaining to a system that is usable by just one person at a time. Although the UNIX system is primarily a multi-user system, it also has a single-user mode that is usually entered just after the system is booted. Single-user mode is usually used for filesystem repair and maintenance and other functions for which the superuser requires exclusive use of the computer. Even when it is in single-user mode, the UNIX system is able to run several processes simultaneously (multiprogramming). Single-user mode is usually terminated by exiting from the single-user shell by either issuing the exit command or striking the end-of-file character. In either case, the demise of the single-user shell wakes up the waiting init process, leading to the execution of the '/etc/rc' script and then multi-user mode.

Sixth Edition   *See* Version 6.

sizeof operator   A C operator that returns the size, in bytes, of its operand. This operator is unique in C because its operand can be either a variable or a type name. For example, the following function call requests a region of storage from calloc that is large enough to store 200 longs. (calloc is a relative of malloc; its first argument is the number of elements to allocate, and its second is the size of each element.)

```
long *p;
. . .
p = calloc(200, sizeof(long));
```

Although sizeof looks like a function call, it actually represents a constant.

sleep

To suspend execution. UNIX processes sleep while waiting for I/O fulfillment, the death of an offspring, or for a specific time interval to elapse. These three sleeps are caused by the I/O system calls, the `wait` system call, and the `sleep` system call, respectively. After the process wakes up, execution resumes from the point at which is was suspended.

A UNIX system call that delays for a fixed period of time.

socket   A communication endpoint in the Berkeley system. Sockets are managed by the kernel so that unrelated processes, including processes on separate machines, can communicate. Berkeley UNIX contains several system calls that relate to sockets, including calls to create sockets, access sockets, and associate specific sockets with particular communication domains. UNIX-domain sockets appear as named files in the UNIX filesystem. They are identified by the letter 's' in the file type character of a long format `ls` listing. The most widely known UNIX-domain socket on Berkeley systems is probably '/dev/lp'. Directing output to '/dev/lp' actually sends it to the print spooler, which then spools the data to the line printer.

software   Programs and programming facilities stored in a computer-accessible medium.

software tool   A simple program that has many uses. Software tools are often combined to build new applications. One UNIX adage claims that a program is a software tool if it has been used for some purpose other than that envisioned by the author of the program. More specific criteria for being a software tool include limited, specific functionality, flexibility of application, and limited size. Most software tools can operate in a pipeline. For example, the `grep` program is an exemplary software tool. It has a limited functionality (searching for text patterns in its input), flexibility (it can search for any pattern that can be specified by a regular expression), it is not a large program, and can be used in a pipeline.

sort key   A specification that tells the sort program how to order the input lines. Typically the sort key contains a primary key, which indicates the most important sort criteria, and secondary keys, which are used when lines compare as equal using the primary keys.

source code   Original version of a program, written in a particular programming language. A compiler transforms source code into object code. The term derives from the fact that source code files are the original (source) files from which the executable versions of a program are derived. Also called code.

source file   A file that contains source code. *See* source code.

source license   A license for a software system that includes the right to have a copy of the program source code. Originally, all UNIX licenses were source licenses. As the system became more commercial, source licenses became expensive and often limited to universities and research institutions. Source licenses are not available for some versions of UNIX. *See also* binary license.

special file   File used as an interface to an I/O device. Special files usually reside in the '/dev' directory and come in two types: block special files for devices that can support filesystems and character special files for everything else. UNIX systems contain at least one special file for each I/O device connected to the computer. There are often more than one per device; for example, some devices (e.g., disks and tapes) support both a character and a block interface, and some devices (e.g., tapes, graphics hardware) support more than one interface protocol. Special files can be accessed with the same I/O system calls that are used to access ordinary files, although many device drivers support additional functionality, which is often accessed via the ioctl system call. *See also* block special file; character special file; device file; I/O device; major device number; minor device number.

spooler   Software for managing access to a printer. Spoolers accept print requests from users, manage the print queues, and send one print job at a time to the printer. The term is derived from the mainframe phrase *simultaneous peripheral operation on-*

line, which was once the technical term to describe printer management software.

spool directory   A directory that contains files that are about to be printed by spooler software.

spreadsheet   A software package that allows the user to place numbers, text, and formulas in a row – column worksheet. In most spreadsheets, all computed values are updated each time any of the spreadsheet's numeric constants are changed.

square bracket   *See* bracket.

stack

A sequential data structure. The most recently stored items are the first removed. Most modern computers contain hardware stack facilities, and most modern languages, such as C, place subroutine return addresses and subroutine local variables on the stack. *See also* push; pop.

To place something on a stack. *See also* push.

stack machine   A computer that makes heavy use of a last-in, first-out storage mechanism. On most stack machines, subroutine linkage information, subroutine parameters, and subroutine local variables are stored on the stack.

stack overflow   A condition that occurs when a program's use of the stack exceeds the storage capacity of the stack. On some systems, C compilers generate code for each function that checks stack usage when the function is invoked, so that the program can detect stack overflow. On other systems stack overflow is detected by the operating system.

stack trace   A record of the contents of a stack, which is often used for debugging.

Stallman, Richard   Developer of emacs, and leader of the GNU (GNU is Not UNIX) project.

standard error The I/O connection where many programs place error messages. One of the three I/O connections opened for programs run by the shell. Associated with file descriptor 2. Also called *stderr*.

standard input Predefined source of input for many programs. One of the three I/O connections opened for programs run by the shell. Associated with file descriptor 0. Also called *stdin*. *See* input redirection.

standard I/O connections An I/O channel that is prepared in advance for a program; these connections can be used without any preliminaries, such as creating a connection using the open system call. The UNIX shell prepares three standard I/O connections for each process that it executes: the standard input, the standard output, and the standard error. The standard channels usually are connected to the user's terminal, but they can be reassigned using the shell's command line I/O redirection facilities. *See also* I/O redirection; input redirection; output redirection; pipeline.

standard I/O library *See* portable C I/O library.

standard output Place to which many programs direct their output. One of the three I/O connections opened for programs run by the shell. Associated with file descriptor 1. Also called stdout. *See also* output redirection.

statement An individual instruction in a programming language.

statements, C C statements are used in the bodies of functions to manage the sequence of instructions. Computations and logical comparisons are performed in expressions, which can be used as statements or as the test expression in iterative and conditional statements.

for	Iteration	switch	One of N way branch
do	Iteration	while	Iteration
break	Exit from loop	continue	Start next loop iteration
compound	Execute several statements as one	return	Exit from subroutine
expression	Perform arithmetic and logical operations	if	Conditional
goto	Goto a statement	null	Do nothing

statements, compound   A group of statements that are treated collectively. Unlike a procedure, which is called (and can be passed arguments, and can return values), a compound statement is simply a syntactic device to allow several statements to be placed in a context where, syntactically, only one statement is appropriate. In C and in the Bourne shell, compound statements are formed by surrounding a group of statements with braces. C compound statements can contain declarations.

statements, conditional

In a programming language, statements that specify alternative processing paths. The specific path that is chosen depends on the value of a control expression. In contrast to an iterative statement, which specifies how many times a given path should be executed.

The Bourne shell contains the if statement, the && and || conditional operators, and the case statement.

The C shell contains the if statement and the case statement.

C contains the if statement and the switch statement. C expressions can contain the conditional operator, which evaluates one of two expressions, based on the value of a control expression.

statements, iterative

In a programming language, statements that specify how many times a given group of statements (called a *loop*) should be executed.

In the Bourne shell, the iterative statements are for, while, and until.

In the C shell, the iterative statements are foreach, repeat, and while.

In C, the iterative statements are for, do, and while.

statements, null   A statement that is necessary syntactically, but that does not do anything. Such statements are common in C programs because of its rich expression syntax. For example, programmers often write iterative statements that perform all their action in the control expression. The following statement repeatedly increments a pointer until it points at a zero, causing the loop to terminate. The body of the loop is a null statement, which is indicated by the semicolon.

```
int *ptr;
. . .
while(*ptr++)
    ;
```

static memory   Memory circuitry that does not need to be periodically refreshed to retain its information. Typical static memory is less dense (fewer storage cells per chip) and more expensive (per bit) than dynamic memory, but faster than dynamic memory. *See also* dynamic memory; memory.

static storage class   *See* storage class, static.

status, process   *See* process status.

stderr   *See* standard error.

stdin   *See* standard input.

stdio library   *See* portable C I/O library

stdout   *See* standard output.

sticky mode   *See* save text mode.

storage class   In C, an attribute that can be applied to a variable definition to control how the variable is stored, and also an attribute that can be applied to a variable or function definition, to control its visibility. Also, typedef is a form of storage class. *See also* storage class, auto; storage class, extern; storage class, register; storage class, static; and storage class, typedef.

storage class, auto   In C, auto is the default storage class within a function (in a local definition). It specifies that the variable should be created when its enclosing block is created and destroyed when control passes out of its enclosing block. auto can be specified only in a local declaration, not in an external declaration. *See also* storage class, register.

storage class, extern   In C, a storage class that specifies a reference to a variable that is defined elsewhere, either in another file or in the same file. The referenced variable is always an external variable, not a local variable. Initializers may not be supplied in an extern declaration because the meaning of extern is that the variable is defined elsewhere. extern is the default storage class in all external declarations, but it may also be used in local declarations to reference external data. When a variable is declared extern outside of any function, then it is visible for the remainder of that source code file. When a variable is declared extern inside of a function, then it is visible throughout its enclosing block.

storage class, register   In C, a variant of the auto storage class that suggests to the compiler that it should store the variable in a register, if possible. You may not take the address of a variable declared as register, and the C compiler is free to allocate the variables outside of a register if a register is not available. *See also* storage class, auto.

storage class, static   In C, a storage class whose meaning depends on where it occurs. When present in a function (in a local declaration), it specifies that the variable should be stored externally (existing for the lifetime of the program) but be accessible only from within the function. Unlike auto variables, static variables are not created each time their enclosing block is activated;

thus there is only one copy of each static variable, even if their enclosing function is called recursively. When static is used in an external declaration, it specifies that the data or function is visible only in the current file; it cannot be accessed by functions that are housed in other files.

storage class, typedef In C, a storage class that is used to define new data types. typedef does not perform the same type of operation as do the other storage classes, but syntactically it is used in the same way as the others; hence it is technically a storage class. Type names created by typedef can be used in the same way as other type names: in casts, in declarations, and as the operand of the sizeof operator.

stream

A modular, full-duplex character processing element, developed by Dennis Ritchie, that regularizes the UNIX kernel's character I/O facilities. Streams are present on later versions of System V.

A sequence of items. UNIX filters often treat their input as a stream, enabling them to work on data sets of unlimited length. In the C language, you can use the getchar and putchar functions to read/write and the standard I/O stream character by character, or you can use the gets and puts functions to read/write the standard I/O line by line.

stream editor A form of text editor that operates on an input stream. Unlike conventional text editors, a stream editor cannot back up or move forward. All it can do it is execute the editing commands on the data as it passes through. sed is the UNIX system's stream editor.

string A sequence of characters; an array of characters. In C, strings are always terminated by a null ('\0') character.

string concatenation To place one string onto the end of another.

string constant In C, a constant whose type is *array of characters*. String constants are enclosed in double quotes (" "), unlike character constants, which are enclosed in single quotes. Like all arrays, the *value* of a string constant is its address. A string constant cannot be assigned to an array, but its location can be assigned to a character pointer variable. When string constants are the initializer in character array definitions, the array is initialized to the value of the string constant. This is the closest that C comes to allowing arrays to be assigned a value (this is not an assignment, because it occurs during compilation, not during execution). By convention, the C compiler inserts a null ('\0 ') at the end of string constants to mark their end.

otringizc In C, a ANSI C preprocessor feature that allows you to create a string from a macro argument. This makes it possible to give an argument to a macro, and have the macro use that argument as a reference to a variable or a function and also use it as a string. In a preprocessor definition, a macro argument is converted to a string by preceding it with a #. For example, the following shows a macro named CHECK that checks to see that a variable is within a certain range. An error message is printed if the variable is not within the range.

```
#define CHECK(v, max, min) do \
    if (v < min || v > max) \
        printf("%s is out of range: %d\n", #v, v); \
    while(0)
```

If this macro is invoked as CHECK(xindex, 0, 99), then the preprocessor will generate the following replacement text

```
do
    if (xindex < 0 || xindex > 99)
        printf("%s is out of range: %d\n", "xindex", xindex);
    while(0)
```

string register A feature of the nroff/troff text formatter that allows a string to be stored for later use in a document. The nroff/troff string registers are loaded (with a string) using the .ds command, and their values can be interpolated into a document using the *(xx or *x commands (where *xx* and *x* represent the name of a string register).

strip   To remove the relocation information and symbol table from an object file. This makes the file smaller, but it makes it more difficult to decipher core dumps and to do other software debugging chores. Executable files can be stripped using the `strip` utility, or by supplying the `-s` command-line option to the C compiler (`cc`) or to to the linkage editor (`ld`).

stripped   An executable file that does not contain relocation information or symbol table.

structure tag   In C, a name that is used to refer to a given type of structure. For example, the following declaration specifies the characteristics of a structure, and specifies that the structure tag `pixel` can be used to declare structures (or pointers to structures) with this type.

```
struct pixel {
    int red, green, blue, alpha;
};
```

This declaration does not create any variables. It only creates a tag (name) for a structure containing three `int`s named `red`, `green`, `blue`, and `alpha`. Given this tagged declaration, the following definition creates a two dimensional array of pixels.

```
struct pixel screen[512][512];
```

See also structure type.

structure type   In C, an aggregate data type whose members are referred to by name. Members may be of any type. Structures are used to package related variables, so that they may be manipulated either individually or as a group. Structure declarations can include a tag, which can subsequently be used to declare additional instances of a structure. *See also* structure tag.

su   A UNIX command that changes temporarily changes the identity of a logged-in user. People who have two separate accounts on a system can use `su` to switch from one account's access privileges to the other's. A common use of `su` is for system administrators to temporarily assume `root` privileges.

subdirectory   Directory below another directory in the filesystem hierarchy. For example, the directory '/usr/bin' is a subdirectory of the '/usr' directory.

subroutine   A set of instructions in a program that performs a given task and is invoked by name.

subtree   A branch of the UNIX filesystem. A subtree consists of a directory and its files, plus its subdirectories and their contents, and so on. Several UNIX utilities operate on all the files in a subtree, including find, du, tar, and cpio.

suffix   *See* extension.

Sun   A manufacturer of computers that run the UNIX system, and one of the major technical forces in the UNIX field, especially in the area of networking.

superblock   The filesystem header. The superblock is the second block of a filesystem and contains information about that filesystem, such as filesystem size, its number of i-nodes, and the location of its free blocks. Each time a filesystem is mounted, the kernel sets aside a block buffer to hold its superblock. *See also* bootblock.

superuser   A special privilege level that exists in the UNIX system to allow system managers to perform certain functions that should not be performed by ordinary users. The superuser is not constrained by the normal file access mode system. *See also* root.

support

From computer professionals, advice, training, referrals, site management, software installation, and other services that make it easier for ordinary users to use a computer system.

From a computer system, the ability to use a particular process, structure, or piece of hardware or software. For example, a compiler might support a machine's floating-point hardware by generating the appropriate instruction sequence. Without that support, floating-point operations would either be disallowed or performed in software. Or, a disk controller might support one manufacturer's disk drive, but not another's.

suspend character   A special keyboard character that can be struck to suspend the current job. The current job will enter a non-executing state, and the current shell will move to the foreground, enabling you to enter shell commands. After suspending a job, you can use bg to cause it to execute in the background or fg to execute it in the foreground. Available only on systems with job control. The suspend character is usually mapped onto the Ctrl-Z key.

suspended   Awaiting continued execution.

SVID   The System V interface definition. A standard developed by AT&T to define compliance of versions of UNIX with their System V standard.

swap space   Region on a mass storage device where processes are stored when they are swapped out. Unlike the storage for ordinary files, which is organized to maximize convenience, information (process images) in swap space is stored contiguously to minimize access time. Swap space is usually many times larger than main memory. For example, a computer with 4 megabytes of main memory might have 30 megabytes of swap space. *See also* save text mode; swapping.

swapping   Temporary storage of an active process on disk. When more processes are active than can simultaneously fit in main memory, some processes that are waiting for their time slice are temporarily moved to swap space. After an interval in swap space, the process will be brought back into main memory so that it can execute. On a heavily loaded system, active processes are continually shuttling between swap space and main memory, and idle processes (e.g., inactive background daemons) spend most of their time in swap space. The act of transferring a process from main memory to mass storage is called *swapping out*; the opposite procedure is called *swapping in.*

switch   *See* option.

switch statement   In C, a multiway branch that transfers control to one of several locations, based on the value of an expression. Each location is identified by a constant expression. Analogous to the Bourne shell's case statement.

symbolic link   A feature on Berkeley UNIX systems that enables one file to reference another file. The referenced file may be either an ordinary file or a directory, and it may be on any filesystem. Symbolic links are created when you supply the -s command-line option to the Berkeley ln command. The kernel creates a symbolic link by allocating space for a file, recording the file's type (symbolic link) in its i-node, and then placing the name of the referenced file into the symbolic link file. When a program opens the symbolic link (for reading or writing), the kernel fetches the symbolic link's contents to discover the name of the referenced file, and then the kernel actually opens the referenced file. In a short format ls listing of a symbolic link, the referenced file is actually displayed, but in a long format listing of a symbolic link the contents of the symbolic link itself are detailed, unless the -L option is supplied.

```
$ ls -l /usr1/john/c/hpsrt.c
-rw-rw---- 1  john  1834  Jan  8 00:19 /usr1/john/c/hpsrt.c
$ ln -s /usr1/john/c_src/hpsrt.c heapsort.c
$ ls -s heapsort.c
    2 heapsort.c
$ ls -l heapsort.c
-rw-rw---- 1   kc    20  Feb  2 13:59 heapsort.c -> /usr1/john/c/hpsrt.c
$ ls -lL heapsort.c
-rw-rw---- 1  john  1834  Jan  8 00:19 /usr1/john/c/hpsrt.c
$ _
```

(Note that -s option of ls lists the size of a file in blocks.) *See also* link.

symbol table   An optional part of object files and executable files that indicates the locations of the procedures and variables in the program image. The compiler usually produces object files containing a symbol table. Symbol tables are necessary for linking a file and for symbolically debugging a file. However, executable files that do not have a symbol table are smaller and more difficult to alter (maliciously). The symbol table can be removed by supplying the compiler option -s, or by using the `strip` command.

sync   To instruct the kernel to flush its memory resident buffers to disk, so that the disk is up to date. The UNIX system contains the `sync` program to sync the kernel. You must perform a sync before halting a UNIX system; otherwise the information in memory resident buffers is lost. System crashes often damage the UNIX filesystem because they stop the processor without performing a sync.

syntax   Rules that govern the construction of sentences in a language. In computers the term *syntax* is used to describe the rules for writing valid statements in programming languages or command languages.

syntax analysis   To decode the syntax of something, such as a computer program. *See also* `yacc`.

syntax error   An error in a program that is caused by breaking the syntactic rules of the language. For example, in a language that requires semicolons at the end of each statement, it would be a syntactical error to omit a semicolon after a statement. In most cases, the compiler or interpreter recognizes the error and prints a diagnostic message. *See also* semantic error.

system   A group of things that work together. For example, the UNIX system is a collection of software (the kernel, the utility programs) that works together with computer hardware to allow people to productively use a computer.

system call   Request by an active process for a service from the UNIX kernel. The UNIX system contains system calls to perform I/O, to control, coordinate, and create processes, and to read and set various status elements (such as the date). *See also* trap.

system generation   Configuring the system software so that it operates with a given set of peripheral devices and default options.

system manager   Person in charge of operating and maintaining a system.

system time   *See* execution time.

System V   AT&T's version of the UNIX system. System V was proclaimed to be the standard UNIX system by AT&T in 1984.

T

tab   An ASCII character code. Most printers or terminals advance the cursor or printhead to the next preset horizontal location when they receive a tab. On terminals that lack a Tab key, you can usually generate a tab by pressing Ctrl-I.

tape   *See* magnetic tape.

tape archive   *See* tar. (*See also* cpio.)

tape drive   A mass storage device that uses magnetic tape to store information. Tape drives can usually operate at high speed if they are accessed sequentially, but they are very slow when accesses are to random locations on the tape.

tar   A UNIX program for reading and writing multiple files stored on a magnetic tape. tar creates a librarylike format on the tape, so that individual files can be retrieved or so that new files can be added to the end of the tape. tar is designed to produce tapes that are easily interchanged between different systems because the header information on the tape is ASCII text. tar is also used to produce ordinary files that have the standard tar librarylike structure, usually so that a group of files can be conveniently sent to another system via some method other than tape transfer, such as by UUCP transport or by network transport. tar is also used on smaller UNIX systems to transfer files via floppy diskettes. The term tar is derived from the phrase tape archive. *See also* magnetic tape; tar tape; cpio.

tar archive   A tape or file in tar format. *See also* tar.

tar tape   A magnetic tape that contains files in a format that can be read by the tar program. *See also* tar.

tbl   An `nroff`/`troff` preprocessor that makes it easier to typeset tables. *See also* `troff`.

TCP   A standard protocol for transferring information, which is often used on UNIX local-area networks such as Ethernets. Supported by the Berkeley networking software. The term *TCP* is an acronym for transmission control protocol.

TCP/IP   A pair of networking protocols. *See* TCP; IP.

tee   A UNIX program that can divert its standard input to files while also copying it to its standard output. Typically used when you want to see a program's standard output on the screen while simultaneously saving it in a file.

```
$ spell wpdoc | tee errwords
besonders
mindestens
teh
versucht
wenig
$ cat errwords
besonders
mindestens
teh
versucht
wenig
$ _
```

teletype   An obsolete form of printing terminal, whose main relevance to the UNIX system is that is the historical source of the UNIX term for a terminal connection (*tty*). *See* printing terminal.

$TERM   A shell variable that contains the name of your terminal. This variable is used by programs such as `vi` that send terminal specific control codes to your terminal.

termcap   A subroutine package that enables programs to generate output that appears at specific locations on the screen of a terminal. The termcap package manages the details of sending the correct escape sequences to various types of terminal to make the output appear in the desired location. The termcap subroutine package gleans information about the proper control codes for

185

each terminal from the '/etc/termcap' terminal capabilities database.

terminal An I/O device consisting of a keyboard plus either a video display device or a printer. Terminals allow users to interact with a computer. Many personal computers contain an integral display/keyboard.

terminal handler The part of the UNIX kernel that manages the data flow to and from terminals. It adapts to the terminal's needs for tab expansion, and so forth. and it can also adapt to the user's desire to use the terminal in a given style. (Also called a *tty handler*.)

terminate To cause the demise of a process.

terminate signal A UNIX signal (number 15) that can be sent to a process to cause its demise. The terminate signal can be caught by a process. *See also* kill signal; interrupt signal; signal.

TEX A text formatter developed by Donald Knuth. Roughly comparable in functionality to `nroff`/`troff`.

text Data that consists primarily of letters, digits, and punctuation symbols, usually divided into lines (or paragraphs). On most UNIX systems, text is coded in the ASCII coding system.

text editor *See* editor, text.

text entry mode An operating mode of many text editors. When the editor is in text entry mode, everything that is typed (with a few exceptions) is added to the edit buffer. Contrast with command mode, during which keyboard entry is interpreted as commands. *See also* modeless; command mode.

text file A file composed solely of ASCII characters that is usually structured into lines.

text formatter A program used to prepare text for final publication or printing. Text formatters smooth margins, align tables, control spacing, position titles, and so on. Most formatters work by interpreting format control codes that are present in the text file. The basic UNIX System text formatting programs are nroff and troff, plus eqn, neqn, tbl, refer, pic, and grap for specialized jobs. Other text formatters that are available for UNIX systems include scribe and TEX. *See also* editor, text.

text region   The region in a process image that contains the instructions of a program. The size of an object file's text segment is displayed by the size program. *See also* data region; BSS region.

text table   A kernel data structure that records the locations of program text that is being shared by several processes.

third party   A supplier of computer equipment or services other than the principal manufacturer of a computer. Such equipment is usually compatible with that provided by the original supplier.

Thompson, Ken   Ken Thompson was the original developer of UNIX, on a DEC PDP-7 minicomputer at Bell Laboratories.

thrashing   A situation in which a computer is constantly accessing information from disk but is accomplishing little or nothing. One cause of thrashing is when a computer needs to simultaneously have two blocks of data resident in memory, but the act of bringing one in from disk always forces the other to be copied back to disk.

tilde substitution   A feature of the Korn shell and the C shell that makes it easier to refer to user's home directories. At the beginning of a word, the pair of characters ˜/ stands for the pathname of the user's home directory, and the sequence *˜name/* stands for the pathname of *name*'s home directory.

```
$ cd
$ pwd
/usr1/kc
$ cd /sys
$ ls ~/.profile
/usr1/kc/.profile
$ ls ~dan/telnos
/usr2/dan/telnos
$ _
```

See also argument list generation.

time and materials   A type of maintenance arrangement where the computer owner pays for service based on the time spent by service personnel and the cost of the parts and supplies.

time-sharing   A technique for sharing a computer and its resources among several tasks, so that each task appears to have exclusive use of the computer. This is accomplished by switching very rapidly from parts of one task to sections of another so that it appears that all of the activities are occurring simultaneously. Most time-sharing system are designed to be used by several users, although the basic capabilities of time-sharing are useful even if just one person is using the machine.

token   A symbol with an agreed on value. Tokens are usually used in situations where two programs, or two routines within a program, are exchanging messages, and the tokens are used in the messages. Contrast with a magic number, which is an unusual value that would not usually appear in a given context. *See also* magic number.

token pasting   In C, a feature of the ANSI C preprocessor that allows two macro arguments to be pasted together to form a new symbol. Two macro arguments separated by ## are pasted together. On pre-ANSI versions of C this feature was often accomplished by separating two macro arguments with a null comment (/**/), but this was never universally portable. Token pasting is often used to create new identifiers, as in the following.

```
#define DECL(a, b, init) int a ## b = init
```

Given this definition, the macro call DECL(xindex, 10, 0); causes the preprocessor to produce the following replacement text.

```
int xindex10 = 0;
```

tool   *See* software tool.

trace   To follow the control flow in an executing program, using a debugger such as adb.

trace, stack   *See* stack trace.

transistor   A semiconductor device that is capable of switching and/or amplifying electrical signals.

transmission control protocol   *See* TCP.

trap

A machine instruction that is often used as the system call interface between ordinary applications software and the kernel software. When an application executes the trap instruction, the kernel takes over. It performs the requested service and then resumes the applications program. *See also* system call.

A feature of the nroff/troff text formatter that allows macros to be invoked automatically when the text formatting process reaches a predetermined vertical position on the page. nroff/troff traps are often used to invoke page header and footer macros, although there are other uses.

tree   A hierarchical system in which connections between two members of equal rank occurs through item(s) of higher rank and in which each member is directly connected to at most one item of higher rank. The UNIX filesystem is tree structured. *See also* subtree.

triple indirect block   A block that contains the addresses of a file's double indirect blocks. The double indirect blocks contain the addresses of the file's indirect blocks, and these in turn contain the addresses of the blocks of the file. Used only for the largest files. *See also* double indirect block; indirect block; i-node; filesystem.

troff   A text formatting program that runs on UNIX systems. `troff` is designed to output to laser printers and typesetters; a compatible program called `nroff` can output to ordinary printers. However, the term `troff` often refers to the entire `troff`-based typesetting system, not just to the program named `troff`. `troff` was first developed by Joseph Ossanna to format documents on a Graphic Systems C.A.T. phototypesetter. Since then the software has been extended by B. W. Kernighan to work, via a printer-specific driver, on any high-resolution printer. The new version's name is `ditroff` (device-independent `troff`), but it is often called `troff`. `troff` documents contain plain text interspersed with control codes that specify the document format. For example, the code `.sp` in a `troff` document requests extra vertical space, and the code `\f2` switches to the current Italic font. `troff` itself is a low-level programming language; most people format their documents using macro packages, which are `troff` language scripts that provide a more convenient, result-oriented capability. The most common UNIX document preparation macro packages are `-ms` (manuscript macros), `-mm` (memorandum macros), `-man` (manual page macros), and `-me` (Eric Allman's macros). One advantage of `troff`'s programmable approach to document formatting is that additional software, known as *preprocessors*, can be created for specialized typesetting tasks. The most common preprocessors are: `eqn`, for typesetting equations; `tbl`, for typesetting tabular data; `refer`, for typesetting references; `pic`, for typesetting line drawings; and `grap`, for typesetting graphs. *Pronounced* tee-roff. *See also* macro package; `-mm`; `-ms`; `-me`; `-man`; `eqn`; `pic`; `refer`; `grap`; `nroff`.

Trojan horse   A program able to create a security loophole by imitating a standard utility program. Trojan horses have the same name as a standard utility program; `ls` is the most common choice. There are several ways to proceed. If an executables directory ('/bin', '/usr/bin', etc.) can be written in by any user, then a Trojan horse can be left there. If the system source code is writable, then Trojan horse source code can be hidden in the source code for a legitimate routine, on the assumption that the routine will eventually be compiled and installed. Another ruse is to leave the Trojan horse in a nonprotected directory and hope that the superuser search string is set to execute software in the current directory. Then when the superuser visits that directory, the Trojan horse program is executed in place of the legitimate software. Once the superuser executes a Trojan horse, it can do anything, from destructive acts, to acts that make it easier to penetrate security at a later date. To protect against the methods mentioned above, you should take the following precautions: restrict write privileges on directories containing executables, restrict access to source code, install software only if it is acquired from legitimate sources, and make sure that the superuser search string never executes software In the current directory. *See also* $PATH; security.

tty   *See* terminal handler.

type   In a programming language, a characteristic of a variable that indicates how big it is, how its binary bit pattern should be interpreted, and what operations may be performed on it. Most languages have built-in types, and many allow programmers to define their own types. Common types represent whole numbers, real (fractional or large) numbers, Booleans, characters, arrays, and groups of data (Pascal records, C structures). *See also* types, C.

type cast   *See* cast operator.

type checking   Checking performed by a compiler to detect possible programmer errors. Different languages have various rules that dictate how types may be combined in expressions. For example, different types in Modula-2 may not be used in a single expression (with minor exceptions). In C, almost any conceivable mixture of types is allowed; the C compiler does its best to perform the required conversions so that the result may be calculated. Modula-2 is said to be strongly typed, while C is weakly typed.

type conversion   Changing data of one type into another, usually so that an expression or an assignment may be performed. For example, to add an integer to a floating-point number, the integer is customarily converted to a floating point number, and then the addition is performed. The conversion is necessary because integers and floating point numbers use different binary representations, and computers do not have hardware that can perform arithmetic on two different types at once. *See also* cast operator.

typedef   In C, a storage class that is used to create new data types from existing types. *See also* storage class, typedef.

types, C   The C language contains the following fundamental data types.

   void   A data type that is used when declaring a function, to indicate that the function does not return a value, or that the function does not take any arguments. void* is a generic pointer.

   char   Storage for a character. Either signed or unsigned.

   short   Storage for a whole number, the same size as an int or smaller. Either signed or unsigned.

   int   Storage for a whole number. The most efficient size for the host machine. Either signed or unsigned.

   long   Storage for a whole number, the same size as an int or larger. Either signed or unsigned.

   float   Storage for a real number. May have a fractional part and an exponent. Always signed. Usually smaller than a double.

   double   Storage for a real number. May have a fractional part and an exponent. Always signed.

   enumeration   Storage for a value that can take on one of a specified list of constant values.

   Many additional types are constructed from these, including pointer types, arrays, structures, unions, and bit fields. *See also* types.

typesetter   A very-high-quality printer. Unlike ordinary printers, typesetters contain various styles and sizes of print, all at high quality. Typically, typesetter resolution is more than 1000 points per inch.

typesetting   Producing documents using a typesetter. The UNIX system contains the `troff` program, which can print documents on most typesetters.

type specifier   In most programming languages, a word (or phrase) that indicates the type of a variable.

U

uid number *See* user id number.

ultraviolet erasable programmable read-only memory (UVEPROM) A type of PROM (programmable read-only memory) whose data can be erased by exposure to ultraviolet light. UVEPROM integrated circuits can be easily identified on circuit boards because of their characteristic transparent cover, which admits the UV light. In contrast to PROMs whose data cannot be erased (or to PROMs whose data is erased by other means).

umask The user's file creation mask. When files are created, the default file access mode may be restricted by the umask.

unary minus A minus sign that denotes the negative of the following part of an expression. For example, the minus sign in the expression x + -10 is a unary minus. In contrast to the common use of minus as a binary operator, in which the minus denotes subtraction. For example, the minus sign in the expression x - 10 is a binary operator. *See also* unary operator.

unary operator An operator that takes only one operand, in contrast to a binary operator, which takes two operands. The most familiar unary operator is probably the unary minus. The C language contains numerous unary operators, including the increment and decrement operators (++, --), the indirection operator (*), the address of operator (&), the sizeof operator, the cast operator, and the unary minus. *See also* binary operator; unary plus; unary minus.

unary plus A plus sign used as a unary operator. For example, in x * +5 the + is a unary plus. In some languages unary plus does nothing. In ANSI C the unary plus is used to control expression grouping.

#undef   A C preprocessor directive that removes a macro definition.

underflow   An arithmetic error that occurs when a floating-point operation yields a value that is too small to be represented (or too small to be represented with the required accuracy) in a floating-point variable. In ANSI C, the unary + operator can be used to force parts of expressions to be evaluated together, a technique that is sometimes used to prevent underflow.

union type   A C data type that is similar to a structure, but each of the members of a union is located in the same place. Thus a union allows you to store various data types in a single location and refer to any one of those types by mentioning the name of that union member. The size of a union is the size of its largest member, unlike a structure whose size is the sum of its members (plus any padding needed for alignment).

UNIX   *See* UNIX system.

UNIX Programmer's Manual (UPM)   A reference document that describes all the specific features of the UNIX system. There are appropriate UPMs for each version of UNIX. The traditional UPM contains eight sections, but only the first, the command reference, and the sixth, games, are used by most users. Within each section the citations are organized alphabetically. Newer versions of the manual are often split into several books, and the traditional numbering is either abandoned or downplayed. Another feature of most UPMs is the permuted index, which lists information topically. Also called the *UNIX User's Manual. See also* permuted index.

UNIX system   A portable, multi-user time-sharing operating system. The UNIX system was first developed by Ken Thompson and Dennis M. Ritchie at Bell Laboratories in the early 1970s. It was then enhanced at many locations, but most notably at the University of California at Berkeley. The seminal paper on UNIX is *The UNIX Time-Sharing System*, by Thompson and Ritchie, published in the July 1974 issue of the *Communications of the ACM* (Association for Computing Machinery). The word *UNIX* is a play on the word Multics, which is an earlier operating system that had a strong influence on the UNIX system.

umask

A program that displays or sets the value of the current file creation access mode mask.

The current file creation access mode mask. The default access mode for files is read-write for all, modified by the umask value.

unlink   A technical term for severing the connection between a directory entry and an i-node. Files can have many names (links), which are often created using the ln command. Each file's link count is stored in its i-node. For files with only a single link (only one name), unlinking simply removes the file, by clearing the directory entry, clearing the i-node, and placing the blocks of the file on the filesystem free list. However, when you unlink a file that has more than one link, only two operations are performed: the directory entry is cleared and the link count in the i-node is decremented. The file itself remains because there are still filenames that refer to it. *See also* link.

unmount

On a UNIX system, to remove a filesystem from the currently mounted set of filesystems. This task is performed by the '/etc/umount' program. Individual files on an unmounted filesystem are inaccessible, although the filesystem itself is available for functions such as backups.

To remove a tape from a tape drive.

unsigned   A data type that can only take on non-zero values. In C, a keyword that can convert one of the standard signed integral types, char (usually signed, but not always), short, int, and long, into an unsigned type.

until statement   In the Bourne shell, an iterative statement that repeatedly executes a command list until a given condition becomes true. *See also* iterative statements; while statement.

uppercase   Pertaining to a letter or word that is capitalized.

USENET   A world-wide network of news and discussion groups on UNIX systems. UNIX systems on USENET communicate via the UUCP software protocol, mostly over dial-up public access telephone lines. Topics include technical subjects such as UNIX and C, and other subjects such as recreation, music, and politics. The USENET is unique in that its administration is decentralized, although some of the most important sites, and some of the principal software developers, have a strong influence on the network.

USENIX   A UNIX users' group.

user   Someone who uses a computer system.

user id number   A number that identifies a user. User id numbers are catalogued in the '/etc/passwd' file, and each file's i-node contains the user id number that identifies the file's owner. When a user is executing a program, that person's user id number and group id number are used to determine access rights to files (unless the program is a set user id or set group id program). Also called a *uid* number or *actual user id* number. *See also* group id number; effective user id; effective group id; set user id mode; set group id mode.

user interface   The part of a software package that accepts commands from a person, and displays information. Some people refer to the command line arguments of a noninteractive program as its user interface, but usually the term is reserved for interactive programs, in which the user engages in a dialogue with the program.

user name   The name assigned to a user; the name that a user enters in response to the UNIX system's login: prompt. Synonymous with login name. *See* login name.

user table   List of information about an active process. Each process's user table is part of its execution image. The kernel can only directly access the user table of the current process. *See also* data structure.

user time   *See* execution time.

/usr/group   A UNIX users group.

usual arithmetic conversions   In C, a set of type conversions that are performed to make operands compatible with each other. Although some operators work differently, in most cases the following steps are performed for each pair of operands. Any char or short is converted to int; any unsigned char or unsigned short is converted to unsigned int, and any float is converted to double. If either operand is double, the other is converted to double. Otherwise, if either operand is unsigned long, the other is converted to unsigned long. Otherwise, if either operand is long, the other is converted to long. Otherwise, if either operand is unsigned, the other is converted to unsigned.

utility   A program or subroutine developed to perform generic data processing tasks. For example, most systems have a sort utility that can order a file of words. Sorting is a generic task that need not be completely reprogrammed each time a slightly different sorting need arises. Instead, sorting programs and sorting subroutines are written more generally, so that they may be applied to a range of tasks.

UUCP

UNIX to UNIX CoPy. A software protocol that was originally developed to help automate software distribution. It has become the standard UNIX protocol for telecommunications between most major UNIX systems.

A UNIX program (uucp) that is the user interface to the UUCP protocol. The actual program that implements the UUCP protocol is uucico. *See also* HoneyDanBer UUCP.

UUCP Network   A wide-area network based on the UUCP software protocol. It links most major UNIX systems throughout the world, mostly via the public telephone system. Routes on the UUCP network must specify the exact sequence of machines required to reach the destination. The user interface programs are uucp, to transfer files to a neighboring site; mail, to send messages to people on other systems; and uux, to execute a job on a neighboring site. Only the mail program can forward files through a series of sites to a distant destination; uucp and uux are limited to transactions with neighbor sites.

UVEPROM   *See* ultraviolet erasable read-only memory.

V

variable, shell   In the UNIX shells, a variable that you can create and use, either in shell scripts or interactively. Shell variable names are preceded by a currency symbol except during assignment operations. Shell variables are either local to the current shell, or exported, which places them into the environment of all of the processes that the shell executes. Some of the standard shell variables are $PATH, $PS1, and $TERM. Shell variables are sometimes called *parameters*.

variable   An object in a program whose value is allowed to change. In most programming languages, each variable has a type that specifies its internal representation and allowable operations. Variables are either created by declaring them (in languages such as Pascal and C), using them (in languages such as the Bourne shell and BASIC), or by dynamically allocating them (also in languages such as Pascal and C). Variables created by declarations or by use have a name, which is used to refer to their value. Variables created dynamically have their location stored in a pointer variable, and their values are accessed indirectly, via the pointer.

variable expression   An expression whose resultant value may vary because at least one operand in the expression is not a constant.

variable substitution   *See* parameter substitution.

VAX   A series of 32-bit computers manufactured by the Digital Equipment Corporation. Important to the UNIX system because they were, during the late 1970s and early 1980s, the machines on which the UNIX system was developed. During this time, versions of UNIX for other machines were usually derived from one of the versions for the VAX computers.

VDT   *See* CRT.

vector graphics   A graphics system where images are created by drawing lines from one point to another, in contrast to a raster graphics system, where individual points on are illuminated. The display of most vector graphics systems contains an electron beam that can illuminate a line between any two points on the face of the display. Curves and letters are drawn on a vector graphics system as a sequence of many short vectors. *See also* raster graphics; graphics controller.

vector processor   A hardware device that can be attached to a computer to accelerate operations on lists of numbers.

Version 6   The first widely distributed version of the UNIX system. It was primitive by today's standards, but it is important because it marked the beginning of widespread interest in the UNIX system.

Version 7   The first modern UNIX system. It introduced numerous features and subsystems that are today considered standard, including the Bourne shell and the `troff` typesetting software.

vi   The most widely distributed UNIX text editor. `vi`, which was developed by Bill Joy while he was at the University of California at Berkeley, is based on the original ed text editor. The two most important personalities of the editor are ex, a line editor, and `vi`, a display editor. While using `vi` it is possible to switch to ex and vice versa. `vi` displays, on the screen, a portion of the file being edited. Changes to the file are immediately shown on the screen. Most `vi` commands are single characters, or short sequences of characters. `vi` is not as configurable as the emacs text editor, but its wide availability and use make it the most common UNIX text editor. *Pronounced* vee-eye. *See also* visual editor.

video display   *See* CRT.

virtual memory   A memory system that gives processes the illusion that they have access to more physical memory than they are actually using. The system copies infrequently used pages of memory out to disk. When the process references a memory page that is not currently present in physical memory, the system suspends the process, automatically brings in the requested page from disk, and then restarts the process. *See also* paging.

visibility   In programming languages, a characteristic of an identifier that determines the locations in a program from which the identifier may be accessed. Some languages, such as Modula-2, have elaborate mechanisms for controlling the visibility of an identifier. In C, the visibility of an identifier is relatively simple. An identifier defined within a function is only visible in that function. An identifier defined externally is, by default, visible throughout a program, unless it is specified as static, in which case it is only visible in the source file where it is defined. Non-static functions defined in one file are visible in other files without explicitly being imported, but non-static external variables from one file are only visible in another if they are explicitly imported, by referencing them in an extern declaration.

visual editor   *See* editor, visual.

VLSI   An integrated circuit that contains over 10,000 circuit elements. VLSI is an acronym for *very large scale integration.*

VMS   An operating system created by the Digital Equipment Corporation for their VAX line of computers. The term *VMS* is an acronym for *virtual memory system.* A version of UNIX called *Eunice* is available to run on VMS systems.

void type   In C, a data type that is used for several specialized purposes. It was introduced in ANSI C to make it possible for compilers to perform more usage checking. In function declarations the void type indicates that the function does not return a value, or that the function does not have arguments. The void type is also used in casts to specify that a given value should be discarded. The type void * is a generic pointer type that is compatible with all other pointer types.

volatile type   In C, a characteristic of a data type that tells the compiler that the defined variable may be modified by actions outside the domain of the compiler. Data that may be modified by an interrupt handler, or hardware values that may change asynchronously, should be declared volatile. Operations involving volatile data are not be optimized by the compiler, and volatile data is not stored in registers. This is an ANSI C feature designed to make it easier to write optimizing compilers that operate correctly even for software such as the UNIX kernel. Before the introduction of the volatile type, the UNIX kernel (and similar software) was usually compiled with optimization disabled, to avoid the problems addressed by the volatile type.

volume   A data storage unit, such as an individual tape or a disk pack.

W

WAN *See* wide area network.

wait *See* sleep.

wakeup

To resume execution after sleeping.

A routine in the kernel that awakens sleeping processes.

Whetstone A standard floating-point benchmark program. It allows one to compare the floating-point performance of computer systems. *See* benchmark.

while statement

In the Bourne shell, an iterative statement that repeatedly executes a command list while a condition is true. *See also* `until`; iterative statements.

In the C language, an iterative statement that repeats a statement (or group of statements) while a given condition is true. The statements are not executed if the condition is initially false. *See also* do statement; iterative statements.

white space Spaces or tabs that are used to separate one word from another. In some applications, newline characters are also considered to be white space.

whole number A number that does not contain a fractional part; a counting number.

wide-area network (WAN)   A network of computers that are far apart. A WAN generally requires connections through the public telephone system or other long-distance information vendor. *See also* network; local-area network (LAN).

widow   In text processing, a line of text that is printed at the bottom of a page, awkwardly separated from following text. A section heading or the first line of a paragraph is called a *widow* when printed at the bottom of a page. *See also* orphan.

wild card   *See* metacharacter.

window   A region of the screen that is used for a particular, usually autonomous, function. Many graphics workstations partition the screen into multiple windows, each of which may be used for a separate purpose. *See also* work stations; X windows.

word processing   Working with textual data on a computer to produce documents. The software components of a word processing system may include a text editing program and a text formatting program; or the two functions may be combined into a single program called a *word processor.*

word processor   A program that manages both the appearance and the content of a document. There isn't a standard UNIX word processor, although numerous word processors are available for UNIX systems. *See also* editor, text; `troff`.

working directory   *See* current directory.

workspace   *See* buffer.

workstation   A computer system designed for use by an individual. Workstations have evolved downward from the minicomputer realms, as opposed to being enhanced personal computers. Thus workstations typically contain a powerful CPU, a large memory, multitasking software, and network interfaces. Although both workstations and personal computers are designed to be used by individuals, the term *workstation* usually refers to a more powerful system. Some workstations contain powerful graphics features and are referred to as *graphics workstations.* Some workstations contain software and hardware that is optimized for artificial intelligence applications and are referred to as *AI workstations.* Workstations are often used by engineers, scientists, and programmers. *See also* windows.

wraparound

During a search command in a text editor, the ability to search forward from the current location to the end of the file, and then (if the target is not yet found) to restart the search from the beginning of a file and search to the current location. (Or to restart a reverse search from the end of the file.)

To display a long line of text on more than one line of the screen instead of failing to display the end of the line.

write   To send data to a file or I/O device.

write permission   Permission for a user's programs to write data to a certain file or to create files in a directory. *See also* file access mode; directory access mode.

write protect   To prevent write access. On many disks, there is a switch or other mechanism that can be used to prevent alteration. The UNIX mount program can write protect a filesystem when it is mounted. UNIX files can be write protected using the chmod program. *See also* access mode.

Writer's Workbench   A group of programs created by Bell Laboratories to provide various facilities for writers.

X

X3J11   The ANSI committee that is responsible for C standardization. *See also* ANSI C.

Xenix   A popular version of UNIX, designed to run on personal computers.

XNS   A networking standard developed by the Xerox corporation.

XOFF/XON   A simple flow control protocol that is often used over serial data links, such as the RS232 lines that connect many terminals to computers. When the receiver's buffers are becoming nearly full, it sends the XOFF character to the sender. The sender then refrains from sending further data until it receives a XON character. *See also* flow control.

X Windows   A windowing graphics software system for workstations that allows programs to conveniently display graphics and to be portable to various manufacturer's workstations. *See also* windows.

Y

yacc   A program that makes it easier to write software that parses command or programming languages. yacc, which stands for *yet another compiler compiler*, reads a tabular description of a language syntax, and then emits a C or Ratfor program to recognize that language. Often used with lex, a program for automatically producing lexical analyzers. *See also* compiler compiler; lex.

Yellow Pages   A network service that implements a distributed database. Although the software is very general, the common use of the yellow pages is to facilitate system management by providing access, via the network, to standard UNIX configuration files such as '/etc/passwd' and '/etc/group'. Part of the Sun networking software.

Z

zeroeth argument *See* command name.

zombie A process that is terminated but whose parent process exists and has not yet acknowledged the child's termination. Zombie processes consume a slot in the process table; thus, an accumulation of zombie processes can eventually be fatal. *See also* orphaned process.

APPENDIX:
STANDARD UNIX FILES
AND DIRECTORIES

. (dot)   A pseudonym for the name of the current directory. Dot is a link to the current directory's common name, which is stored in the parent directory. *Pronounced* dot. *See also* directory . .

.. (dot dot)   A pseudonym for the name of the parent directory. Dot dot is used in pathnames that ascend the file system. For example, the pathname `../bin/wcfix` is a pathname that starts in the current directory, ascends to the parent directory, and then descends to the 'wcfix' file in the 'bin' directory. The entry dot dot in the current directory is a link to the parent directory. *Pronounced* dot dot. *See also* directory, .. .

.cshrc   A file C shell commands that, if it is present in a C shell user's home directory, is executed each time a C shell is spawned, before the ordinary commands are executed. Note that these commands are executed both for login C shells and for other C shells.

.exrc   A file of `ex/vi` commands that is executed each time you start the `ex/vi` editor, before interactive commands are executed. This file may reside in your home directory, or in the current directory.

.login   A file of C shell commands that, if it is present in a C shell user's home directory, is executed each time a C shell user logs in, before interactive commands are executed.

.logout   A file of C shell commands that, if it is present in a C shell user's home directory, is executed each time a C shell user logs out. Must be in the user's home directory.

.profile   A file of Bourne shell commands that, if it is present in a user's home directory, is executed each time a Bourne shell user logs in, before interactive commands are executed. Commands in

'.profile' are often used to initialize shell variables (e.g., the search string), set the terminal handler's modes, and so on.

a.out   The default name for executable files produced by the C compiler. The –o C compiler command-line option is used to specify an alternate name for the output file.

core   The name of the file produced when a process terminates abnormally and the kernel produces a process image file for debugging. Production of the file is imminent when you see the message ... *core dumped.*

dead.letter   The standard file in which your outgoing messages are saved when the mail program is unable to find the recipients that you have mentioned on the command line.

lost + found   A directory that should be present in the root directory of every file system, so that orphaned files can be placed there by fsck. It is automatically created when file systems are created and, although it is normally empty, it should not be removed.

nohup.out   When processes are executed by nohup (so that they ignore the hangup signal), their standard output is placed into 'nohup.out' unless it has been explicitly redirected to another file.

mon.out   A file into which timing information is placed by the monitoring subroutines of a profiled program, so that a timing summary can be displayed by the prof program.

/   The root directory. The starting point for absolute pathnames.

/bin   On most UNIX systems, the directory containing the most frequently used commands. On many systems only these commands, plus the commands in '/etc', are available in single user mode. Thus the '/bin' directory must contain all of the important system maintenance commands.

/dev   The directory where block special and character special files are usually located.

/dev/console   The character special file for the system console (the operator's terminal).

/dev/mem /dev/kmem   Character special files that allow the user to access the computer's main memory. The '/dev/mem' file accesses absolute locations, whereas the '/dev/kmem' character special file accesses memory from the perspective of the kernel's memory mapping.

/dev/null   A character special file that emulates the null device. Output sent to '/dev/null' is discarded. Attempting to read from '/dev/null' leads to an immediate end of file.

/dev/tty   The character special device handler that performs generic terminal management, such as management of erase and kill characters, management of tabs, and so forth. A program can always open '/dev/tty' to access the controlling terminal, even after I/O redirection. '/dev/tty' should not be confused with the names of the special files used to access individual communications lines, which are often named '/dev/tty00', and similar.

/etc   The UNIX system directory containing files used for system administration.

/etc/group   A file that lists all the groups on a system and lists the users who are members of each group.

/etc/motd   A text file that contains the message of the day. It is typically used by system administrators on larger systems for notices. It is usually displayed each time the user logs in.

/etc/passwd   A text file containing the login information for each user. Each line details the information for a single user, including the encrypted password, the login name, the full name, the user id number, the group id number, the home directory, and the login shell.

/etc/profile   A text file containing Bourne shell commands that is executed each time a Bourne shell user logs in.

/etc/rc   The system startup command script. It contains the commands that the UNIX system performs when it initiates multi-user activity.

/etc/termcap   The database of termcap entries. This file details the terminal control codes for each terminal that can be used by programs such as vi. This file is a huge text file that is searched sequentially each time a termcap entry must be retrieved. Thus the entries should be arranged so that the common terminals on your system are near the front. *See also* '/usr/lib/terminfo'.

/etc/ttys   A text file that details the default baud rate and the status (on or off) of each terminal line. This file is read by init to maintain the multi-user state of the system.

/etc/utmp   A text file containing a list of the currently logged-on users. This file is the major source of information for the who program.

/lib   A directory that contains programming language libraries, such as the standard C subroutine library '/lib/libc.a'.

/mnt   A spare directory that is used as a mount point for miscellaneous file systems.

/sys   A directory that often contains the kernel source code directories.

/tmp   A directory that contains most temporary files.

/unix   The file that contains the UNIX operating system kernel. The name varies; for example, this file is named '/vmunix' on Berkeley systems and '/xenix' on Xenix systems.

/usr   General-purpose directory that is the head of a subtree containing most of the UNIX system software and documentation.

/usr/adm   A directory that contains miscellaneous administrative files and error message logs.

/usr/adm/messages   A log of system error messages.

/usr/adm/wtmp   A record of logins since the file was created. Must be periodically pruned on active systems.

/usr/bin   A directory that contains the less frequently accessed UNIX system utility programs. On most systems, commands in '/usr/bin' are not available during single-user mode, unless the filesystem containing '/usr/bin' is manually mounted.

/usr/dict/words   A list of correctly spelled words. You can access words in the list using the Berkeley look command. For example, the command look gram prints a list of words that start with the letters *gram*.

/usr/games   A directory that contains the game software and sub-directories.

/usr/include   A directory that contains standard C language include files.

/usr/include/sys   A directory that contains the UNIX header files for systems programming.

/usr/lib   A directory that contains many files that are not directly executed by users, plus subdirectories that are used by applications programs. Most of the files and directories stored here are accessed by programs in '/bin' or '/usr/bin'.

/usr/lib/cron   A directory that contains files used by the cron daemon.

/usr/lib/crontab   The task file used by the cron daemon.

/usr/lib/tags   A file that contains a tags database for the kernel software.

/usr/lib/terminfo   A directory that contains the terminfo directories. *See also* '/etc/termcap'.

/usr/lib/tmac   A directory that contains nroff/troff macro packages and related files.

/usr/lib/uucp   A directory that contains the UUCP configuration files, plus the background UUCP programs.

/usr/local   A directory that often contains locally developed software, or software that was acquired independently of the standard Unix distribution.

/usr/local/bin   A directory that often contains locally developed executable files.

/usr/local/lib   A directory that performs the functions of '/usr/lib' for locally developed software.

/usr/man   The directory that contains the manual citation subdirectories.

/usr/pub   A directory that contains miscellaneous public access files.

/usr/pub/ascii   An ASCII table.

/usr/spool   A directory that contains subdirectories for all the programs that need spool directories, such as UUCP and the line printer.

/usr/src   A directory that contains the standard source code directories.

/usr/sys   A common home for system source code and configuration files.

/usr/tmp   A secondary directory for temporary files.

/usr1 /usra /users /home /a   Common places to put user's home directories.